as in word

What your country is going to do
for you — Ask what you can do
for your country — my fellow
citizens of the world. ask not

or other

what America will do for you —

yours, your

Ask rather what you can do
for freedom. Mark of you —
the same high standards of
sacrifice and strength of heart
and will that we seek from
you. ~~That~~ ~alliances~ of

~~rice & progress~~ will be forged

KENNEDY'S LAST DAYS

The Assassination
That Defined a Generation

BILL O'REILLY

SQUARE
FISH

HENRY HOLT AND COMPANY

NEW YORK

An Imprint of Macmillan
175 Fifth Avenue
New York, NY 10010
mackids.com

Square Fish books may be purchased for business or promotional use. For information on bulk purchases,
please contact the Macmillan Corporate and Premium Sales Department at (800) 221-7945 x5442
or by e-mail at specialmarkets@macmillan.com.

Permission to use the following images is gratefully acknowledged (additional credits are noted with
captions): i: JFK Presidential Library and Museum; ii: © Bettmann/Corbis; iii: © Tom Dillard/Dallas
Morning News/Corbis; iv-v: © iStock.com; vi-vii: © Corbis; 1: JFK Presidential Library and Museum; 45: JFK
Presidential Library and Museum; 100: © Wong Yu Liang/Shutterstock.com; 157: JFK Presidential Library and
Museum; 241: JFK Presidential Library and Museum; 246-47: © Bettmann/Corbis; 285-89: © Shutterstock.com
and iStock.com; 334: JFK Presidential Library and Museum

Library of Congress Cataloging-in-Publication Data
O'Reilly, Bill.
Kennedy's last days : the assassination that defined a generation / Bill O'Reilly.
     pages   cm
Includes bibliographical references and index.
ISBN 978-1-250-06042-6 (paperback) / ISBN 978-0-8050-9974-4 (ebook)
1. Kennedy, John F. (John Fitzgerald), 1917-1963—Assassination—Juvenile literature.   I. Title.
E842.Z9O74 2013   973.922092—dc23   2013009026

Originally published in the United States by Henry Holt and Company
First Square Fish Edition: 2015
Book designed by Meredith Pratt
Square Fish logo designed by Filomena Tuosto

10 9 8 7 6 5 4 3 2 1

AR: 7.9 / LEXILE: 1050L

This book is dedicated to my ancestors,
THE KENNEDYS
OF YONKERS, NEW YORK:
hardworking, generous, and honest folk.

CONTENTS

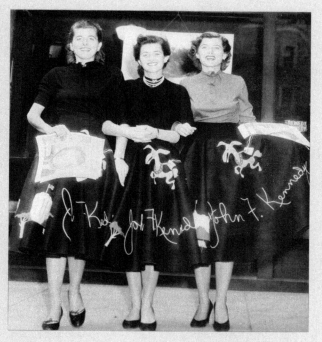

John's sisters Patricia, Jeanne, and Eunice show their support during Kennedy's senatorial campaign. The donkey is a symbol of the Democratic Party. [© Bettmann/Corbis]

"The stories of past courage can define that ingredient—they can teach, they can offer hope, they can provide inspiration. But they cannot supply courage itself. For this each man must look into his own soul."

—John Fitzgerald Kennedy

"It can be said of him, as of few men in a like position, that he did not fear the weather, and did not trim his sails, but instead challenged the wind itself, to improve its direction and to cause it to blow more softly and more kindly over the world and its people."

—E. B. White

PROLOGUE

THE BAD NEWS ARRIVED in religion class. We were in Brother Carmine Diodati's room that day when the radio report came over the loudspeaker: *President John F. Kennedy has been shot in Dallas, Texas, and taken to the hospital.* A short time later, we would learn that he was dead.

We were startled. No one knew what to say. I remember exactly where I was when I heard the news, and so do most Americans who were born before 1953. I'll bet there is someone in your family who can tell you what it felt like to hear the awful news that the president had been assassinated.

Chaminade High School, where I was a freshman, was (and still is) all boys, or "young men," as we were called, so there weren't a lot of tears then. The days that followed were filled with sadness and confusion. We had to go to several sorrowful masses and listen to lectures

The author's ID for Chaminade High School, 1965–66.

about the slain president and the tragedy that had befallen America.

Mostly, we were confused. My life at the time revolved around sports and friends. I didn't think too much about national politics. I took pride in wearing the red and gold school colors on the field, did my homework, and tried to stay in line with the school rules. I don't remember talking to my friends about the assassination.

Life was pretty simple in those days. For adults the rules seemed to be these: You worked, obeyed the law, cared for your family, looked out for your neighbors, and respected your country. The Kennedy assassination shattered that calm sense of order. People throughout America were asking themselves and one another why it happened and who really killed the president.

In 1960, when Kennedy was elected, I was in sixth grade at St. Brigid's Catholic School. Of course his picture was soon on the walls because he was the country's first Catholic president. And he was Irish, too. I had Kennedys in my background. My mother's grandmother was Winifred Kennedy, and all American Kennedys liked to think they were related to this groundbreaking president. And because we were Irish Catholic, too, our family felt deep emotional ties to the president and his family.

Soon after Kennedy was elected, there was a scary change at school. Three months after the inauguration, there was a standoff with Russia and Cuba, and people were afraid there would be a nuclear war. To prepare for this, we had fallout-shelter drills at school. When the bell rang, all the kids had to file out to the school

The Kennedys with Jackie's sister's family, Christmas Eve, 1962. The black dog is Clipper. Mrs. Kennedy is holding Charlie. [JFK Presidential Library and Museum]

parking lot. If a war had started, buses would take us to an underground bunker.

There would be other showdowns during Kennedy's presidency, as well as times of family relaxation. And it seemed as if we were in on them all. There were photos of the president in meetings, walking with world leaders, speaking around the world, sailing on his yacht, and playing with his children. He was a glamorous figure, young and energetic. He had style, and his wife, Jackie, had even more. Kennedy was friendly with the press and let them show what his life was like. He was our first president who liked to be on television.

And it was television that kept the country in touch when he was killed. After the assassination, my mother and father, like most Americans, were glued to the TV. For three days after the 1:40 P.M. news bulletin on November 22, 1963, the country watched. Walter Cronkite, the most respected man in television news, had broken into the broadcast of a soap opera to announce the shooting. All the major networks showed the return of the president's body to Washington, D.C., his funeral mass at the Cathedral of St. Matthew, and his burial in Arlington National Cemetery. Not a single commercial was aired during those three days.

My father was not enthusiastic about the new president, Lyndon Johnson. My mother was sad and mostly worried about Jackie Kennedy and her two young children. To me, Kennedy was a distant figure who died in a terrible way, although many of the photographs of that day have stayed with me always.

It wasn't until I got to college that I began to be interested in politics and in how great men like John Kennedy met the challenges that were thrown at them.

Bill O'Reilly

New York
June 2013

CAROLINE KENNEDY

JOSEPH KENNEDY JR.

KEY PLAYERS

EDWARD KENNEDY

JOSEPH KENNEDY SR.

PRESIDENT JOHN F. KENNEDY AND FAMILY

Caroline Kennedy: Daughter of the president and first lady.

Edward "Ted" Kennedy: Younger brother of JFK, U.S. senator.

Jacqueline "Jackie" Bouvier Kennedy: Wife of JFK, first lady of the United States.

John Fitzgerald Kennedy: World War II hero, Pulitzer Prize–winning historian, U.S. congressman and senator, 35th president of the United States.

John Kennedy Jr.: Son of the president and first lady.

Joseph Kennedy Jr.: Older brother of JFK, U.S. Navy land-based bomber pilot during World War II.

Joseph Kennedy Sr.: Patriarch of the Kennedy family, former U.S. ambassador to Great Britain.

Robert Francis Kennedy: Younger brother of JFK, U.S. senator, U.S. attorney general, candidate for president in 1968.

JACQUELINE BOUVIER KENNEDY

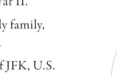
ROBERT FRANCIS KENNEDY

JOHN FITZGERALD KENNEDY

McGEORGE BUNDY

PRESIDENT KENNEDY'S CABINET AND ADVISERS

McGeorge Bundy: JFK's national security adviser.

Lyndon Baines Johnson: JFK's vice president, then 36th president of the United States.

JOHN KENNEDY JR.

xiv ✧

LYNDON BAINES JOHNSON

Robert S. McNamara: Secretary of defense.

Kenneth "Kenny" P. O'Donnell: Organizer of JFK's 1960 presidential campaign, special assistant and appointments secretary to President Kennedy, later campaign manager for Robert Kennedy's 1968 presidential campaign.

David "Dave" Francis Powers: Special assistant and assistant appointments secretary to President Kennedy, later curator of the JFK Library and Museum.

Pierre Salinger: White House press secretary.

Arthur Schlesinger Jr.: Special assistant to the president.

Ted Sorensen: Special counsel to the president.

Earl Warren: Fourteenth chief justice of the Supreme Court, chairman of the President's Commission on the Assassination of President Kennedy, informally known as the Warren Commission.

POLITICAL LEADERS

Fidel Castro: Prime minister and later president of Cuba.

John Connally: Governor of Texas, rides in the presidential limousine in Dallas.

Dwight Eisenhower: Thirty-fourth president of the United States.

Andrei Gromyko: Soviet foreign minister.

Nikita Khrushchev: Premier of the Soviet Union.

Martin Luther King Jr.: Minister, activist leader of the civil rights movement, and later Nobel Peace Prize recipient.

Richard Nixon: President Eisenhower's vice president, presidential candidate against Kennedy.

Harry Truman: Thirty-third president of the United States.

George Wallace: Governor of Alabama.

SECRET SERVICE, FBI, AND POLICE

U. E. Baughman: Head of the Secret Service.

Arnold J. Brown: Texas-based FBI agent who investigates Lee Harvey Oswald and his mother.

Jesse Curry: Dallas police chief.

John Fain: Texas-based FBI agent who investigates Lee Harvey Oswald.

Bill Greer: Secret Service agent driving the presidential limousine.

Clint Hill: Secret Service agent in charge of Jackie Kennedy's detail.

J. Edgar Hoover: Director of the Federal Bureau of Investigation of the United States.

James Hosty Jr.: FBI's expert on Lee Harvey and Marina Oswald.

Roy Kellerman: Secret Service agent protecting JFK.

Winston G. Lawson: Secret Service special agent in charge of organizing JFK's travel protection.

J. D. TIPPIT

ROBERT OSWALD

Eugene "Bull" Connor: Birmingham, Alabama, public safety commissioner.

J. D. Tippit: Officer of the Dallas police force who is killed by Oswald.

LEE HARVEY OSWALD, FAMILY, AND ACQUAINTANCES

GEORGE DE MOHRENSCHILDT

RUTH PAINE

George de Mohrenschildt: Russian-American businessman who helps the Oswalds.

Lee Harvey Oswald: U.S. Marine, defector to the Soviet Union, assassin of Kennedy.

Marguerite Oswald: Mother of Lee Harvey Oswald.

Marina Prusakova Oswald: Wife of Lee Harvey Oswald.

Robert Oswald: Lee Harvey Oswald's older brother.

Ruth Paine: Friend of Marina Oswald.

LEE HARVEY OSWALD

WALTER CRONKITE

OTHERS

Walter Cronkite: CBS newsman who first announces the shooting of the president.

Jack Ruby: Nightclub owner who kills Lee Harvey Oswald.

Edwin Anderson "Ted" Walker: Major general in the U.S. Army, assassination target of Oswald.

Sterling Wood: Boy who testifies that he saw Oswald at the rifle practice range.

MARGUERITE OSWALD

JACK RUBY

MARINA PRUSAKOVA OSWALD

EDWIN ANDERSON WALKER

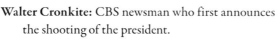

THE MAKING OF A HERO

Kennedy places his hand on an 1850 edition of the Bible brought from Ireland by his ancestors. [JFK Presidential Library and Museum]

CHAPTER ONE

JANUARY 20, 1961

Washington, D.C. 12:51 P.M.

THE MAN WITH FEWER THAN THREE YEARS to live places his left hand on the Bible.

Earl Warren, chief justice of the United States Supreme Court, stands before him reciting the Presidential Oath of Office. "You, John Fitzgerald Kennedy, do solemnly swear . . ."

"I, John Fitzgerald Kennedy, do solemnly swear," the new president repeats in his Boston accent.

John Kennedy was born into wealth and has a refined manner of speaking that would seem to distance him from many people. But he is an enthusiastic and easily likable man. He won the popular vote over Richard Nixon by a razor-thin margin, getting just 49 percent of the total votes. So not everyone loves JFK, but this is an exciting moment for the country.

". . . that you will faithfully execute the office of president of the United States . . ."

"...that I will faithfully execute the office of president of the United States...."

Eighty million Americans are watching the inauguration on television. Twenty thousand more are there in person. Eight inches of thick, wet snow have fallen on Washington, D.C., overnight. Spectators wrap their bodies in sleeping bags, blankets, thick sweaters, and winter coats—anything to stay warm.

The Marine Band stands in front of the Capitol during the inauguration ceremonies. [JFK Presidential Library and Museum]

But John Kennedy ignores the cold. He has even removed his overcoat. At age 43, JFK exudes fearlessness and vigor. His lack of coat, top hat, scarf, or gloves is intentional—this helps to confirm his athletic image. He is trim and just a shade over six feet tall, with greenish-gray eyes, a dazzling smile, and a deep tan, thanks to a recent vacation in Florida.

". . . and will to the best of your ability . . ."

". . . and will to the best of my ability . . ."

In the sea of dignitaries and friends all around him, there are three people vital to Kennedy. The first is his younger brother Bobby, soon to be appointed U.S. attorney general. The president values him for his honesty and knows that Bobby will always tell him the truth, no matter how brutal it may be.

Behind the president is the new vice president, Lyndon Baines Johnson, who is often called LBJ. It can be said, and Johnson himself believes, that Kennedy won the presidency because Johnson was on the ticket, which allowed them to win the most votes in Johnson's home state of Texas.

Finally, the new president glances toward his young wife, standing behind Justice Warren. Jackie's eyes sparkle. Despite her happy face today, Jackie Kennedy has already known tragedy during their seven years of marriage. She miscarried their first child, and the second was a stillborn baby girl. But she has also enjoyed the birth of two healthy children, Caroline and John Jr., and the stunning rise of her dashing young husband from a Massachusetts politician to president of the United States.

John F. Kennedy takes the oath of office, administered by Chief Justice Earl Warren. [© Bettmann/Corbis]

". . . preserve, protect, and defend the Constitution of the United States."

". . . preserve, protect, and defend the Constitution of the United States."

Kennedy's predecessor, Dwight Eisenhower, stands near Jackie. Behind Kennedy stand Richard Nixon, Eisenhower's vice president and Kennedy's adversary in the presidential campaign, and Harry Truman, the Democratic president who held office before Eisenhower.

Normally, having just one of these dignitaries at an event means heightened security. Having all of them at the inaugural, sitting together, is a security nightmare.

The Secret Service is on high alert. Its job is to protect the president. The leader of the service, Chief U. E. Baughman, has been in charge since Truman was president. His agents scan the crowd, nervous about the proximity of the huge audience. One well-trained fanatic with a pistol could kill the new president, two former presidents, and a pair of vice presidents with five crisp shots.

". . . So help you, God."

". . . So help me, God."

The oath complete, Kennedy shakes Chief Justice Warren's hand, then those of Johnson and Nixon and finally Eisenhower.

Kennedy is the youngest president ever elected. Eisenhower is one of the oldest. The great divide in their ages also represents two very different generations of Americans—and two very different views of America. Those watching in person and those watching on TV agree: The future looks limitless and bright.

Now the 35th president of the United States turns toward the crowd. At the podium bearing the presidential seal, Kennedy looks down at his speech.

Kennedy is a Pulitzer Prize–winning historian, having received the award for his book *Profiles in Courage*. He knows the value of a great inaugural address. For months, he has worked over the words he is about to recite. That morning, he rose after just four hours of sleep and, pencil in hand, reviewed his speech again and again and again.

His words resonate like a psalm. "Let the word go forth from this time and place, to friend and foe alike, that the torch has been passed to a new generation of Americans—born in this

Kennedy's inaugural address is one of the shortest in history: thirteen minutes, fifty-nine seconds. [© Associated Press]

After the inauguration, the new president watches the parade pass. The press corps capture every moment. Seated next to Jackie Kennedy is the new president's father. Vice President Lyndon Johnson stands next to President Kennedy. [JFK Presidential Library and Museum]

century, tempered by war, disciplined by a hard and bitter peace, proud of our ancient heritage. . . ."

This is no ordinary inaugural address. This is a promise. America's best days are still to come, Kennedy is saying, but only if we all pitch in to do our part. "Ask not what your country can do for you," he commands, his voice rising to deliver the defining sentence, "ask what you can do for your country."

The address will be hailed as an instant classic. In fewer than 1,400 words, John Fitzgerald Kennedy defines his vision for the nation. He now sets the speech aside, knowing that the time has come to fulfill the great promise he has made to the American people. He must manage the issue with Cuba and its pro-Soviet leader, Fidel Castro. He must tackle problems in a faraway land known as Vietnam, where a small band of U.S. military advisers is struggling to bring stability to a region long rocked by war. And here at home, the civil rights movement requires immediate attention. Tempers in the South are flaring as more and more people demand equal treatment under the law for all races.

JFK surveys the adoring crowd, knowing that he has much work to do.

What he does not know is that he is on a collision course with evil—a course that will cut short the time he has to fulfill the promises he just made.

───

About 4,500 miles away, in the Soviet city of Minsk, an American who did not vote for John F. Kennedy is fed up. Lee Harvey Oswald, a former U.S. Marine Corps sharpshooter, has had enough of life in this communist nation.

Oswald is a defector. In 1959, at age 19, the slightly built, somewhat handsome drifter decided to leave the United States of America, convinced that his political beliefs would make him welcome in the Soviet Union. But things haven't gone according to plan. Oswald had hoped to attend Moscow University, even though he never graduated from high school. In-

Lee Harvey Oswald in a U.S. Marine uniform, in 1956. [© Corbis]

stead, the Soviet government shipped him to Minsk, where he has been working in an electronics factory. Oswald left the United States because he believes in workers' rights and thinks that workers in the United States are treated like slaves, but these endless days in the factory don't make him feel that he has any rights at all.

He was briefly important when his defection was reported by American newspapers. It was extremely unusual for a U.S. Marine to violate the *Semper Fi* (Always Faithful) oath and go over to the enemy. But now, here in Russia, he is anonymous, which he finds unacceptable. Lee Harvey Oswald needs to be noticed and appreciated.

Defection doesn't seem like such a good idea anymore, Oswald confides to his journal.

As America celebrates Kennedy's inauguration, he writes to the U.S. embassy in Moscow. His note is short and to the point: Lee Harvey Oswald wants to come home.

The 1959 photograph Oswald attached to his application for Soviet citizenship.
[© Associated Press]

CHAPTER TWO

1961
United States of America

THE COUNTRY LEE HARVEY OSWALD wants to come home to in 1961 is different in many ways from the country he left in October 1959. President Eisenhower had served for almost the whole decade, from 1953 until 1961. He was the general in command of the winning forces in World War II and is famous around the world. He and his wife, Mamie, are grandparents. Americans trusted him to keep the world safe.

But beginning in 1960, another face appeared on the political scene, that of a young man who is also a war hero. A man who has two small children who sometimes go with him on trips. His glamorous wife wears designer clothes. She took the popular pageboy hairstyle and flipped up the ends to create a lighthearted, fun look. As the bells ring for 1961, it seems as if the country is ready for change.

Change is happening in all parts of life. Things that will one day be familiar make their appearance that year: the first

The Pillsbury Doughboy floats over New York City fifty years after it was introduced. [Debby Wong/Shutterstock.com]

Hardee's restaurant opens in Rocky Mountain, North Carolina. The founder of Weight Watchers holds her first meeting. The "Poppin' Fresh" Pillsbury Doughboy is introduced. The first Six Flags adventure park opens. Johnson & Johnson's Tylenol for adults, Pampers, Life cereal, and Sprite are on grocery shelves. People on the cutting edge of technology are buying the newly invented electric toothbrush. And skateboarding, invented by California surfers, increases in popularity across the country.

Young people's tastes begin to influence fashion. After 15 years of quiet colors, people want to be bright. Jackie Kennedy is a leading example of that trend. She loves intense colors and wears bright pink, yellow, orange, and red.

Youthful tastes are also reflected on the charts: The most popular songs in 1961 are "Let's Twist Again" by Chubby Checker, "Runaway" by Del Shannon, "Surrender" by Elvis Presley, and "Hello Mary

The earliest official portrait of the new first lady. [LOC, USZ62-21796]

Three famous stars—Conway Twitty, Chubby Checker, and Dick Clark—do the Twist. [© Bettmann/Corbis]

Lou" by Ricky Nelson. A movie ticket costs about a dollar, and lines form for the original *Parent Trap, 101 Dalmatians,* and the best movie of the year, *West Side Story.*

Teens have portable record players, small square boxes that play vinyl singles. They dance the Pony to Chubby Checker singing "Pony Time"; they think about consequences when the Shirelles

Rita Moreno dances in her role as Anita in West Side Story. [© CinemaPhoto/Corbis]

sing "Will You Love Me Tomorrow?"; and they dream of dark, dangerous boys as Elvis sings "Surrender."

Communication is improving, too. Half the people in the country can dial long distance directly, without asking an operator to connect them. Although color television is a rarity, 90 percent of people in the United States own black-and-white TVs. In 1961, the first animated weekly prime-time TV show, *The Flintstones*, inspires people to go around saying "Yabba-Dabba-Doo!" Another big hit is *Mister Ed*, featuring a talking horse.

Television was a crucial factor in the election of November 1960.

Presidential debates were broadcast for the first time during the campaign. People saw the young, confident John Kennedy squaring off with the seemingly anxious Richard Nixon. They chose Kennedy's youth and passion at the polls.

The most popular names for children born in 1961 are Michael, David, and John for boys, and Mary, Lisa, and Susan for girls. Famous faces born that year include George Clooney, Meg Ryan, Michael J. Fox, Elizabeth McGovern, Eddie Murphy, and a man who someday will also sit behind the desk in the Oval Office, Barack Obama.

Televised debates offered people their first look at the candidates in face-to-face competition. [© Corbis]

CHAPTER THREE

JANUARY 1961
Washington, D.C.

THE NEW PRESIDENT HAS A COCONUT SHELL on his desk in the Oval Office. It's now encased in plastic with a wood bottom. His staff made sure to put it in a prominent place when they moved him in. The unusual paperweight is a reminder of a now-famous incident that tested John Kennedy's courage and made him a hero.

August 2, 1943
Blackett Strait, Solomon Islands
2:00 A.M.

Eighteen years earlier, in the South Pacific Ocean, three American patrol torpedo (PT) boats were cruising the Blackett Strait, hunting Japanese warships. It was 19 months since the United States had entered World War II. There were more than 50 countries involved in the war now. Since 1939, German leader

Adolf Hitler had been waging his campaign of terror across Europe. In 1937, Japan had attacked China. In 1935, Italy's Mussolini had invaded Ethiopia. These events had divided the countries of the world into two groups—the Allies, led by the United States, Britain, France, and the Soviet Union, and the Axis countries, led by Germany, Italy, and Japan. The United States had entered the war after the Japanese attacked Pearl Harbor, a naval base in Hawaii, on December 7, 1941. By the time the conflict ended in 1945, it was the deadliest and costliest war ever fought.

That night, one small PT boat would come close to being another casualty. At 80 feet long, with hulls of two-inch-thick mahogany and propelled by three powerful engines, these patrol boats were nimble vessels. They were capable of flitting in close to Japanese battleships and launching torpedoes. Those weapons would zoom underwater toward their targets and explode when they hit, sinking the Japanese ships.

John Fitzgerald Kennedy, the skipper of the PT boat bearing the number 109, was a twenty-six-year-old second lieutenant. He slouched in his cockpit, half-awake and half-asleep. He had shut down two of his three engines so they wouldn't make ripples in the water that Japanese spotter planes could see. The third engine idled softly, its deep propeller shaft causing almost no movement in the water. He gazed across the black ocean, hoping to locate the two other nearby PTs. But they were invisible in the darkness—just like *PT-109*.

Lieutenant Kennedy on PT-109. [JFK Presidential Library and Museum]

The skipper didn't see or hear the Japanese destroyer *Amagiri* until it was almost too late. The destroyer was part of the Tokyo Express, a bold Japanese experiment to transport troops and weapons in and out of the tactically vital Solomon Islands using ultrafast warships. The Express relied on speed and the cover of night to complete these missions. *Amagiri* had just dropped 900 soldiers on nearby Kolombangara Island and was racing back to Rabaul, New Guinea, before dawn would allow American bombers to see and destroy it. The ship was longer than a football field but only 34 feet across. This long, narrow shape allowed it to knife through the sea at an astonishing 44 miles per hour.

In the bow of *PT-109*, Ensign George "Barney" Ross was stunned when, through his binoculars, he saw the *Amagiri* just 250 yards away, bearing down on *109* at full speed. He pointed into the darkness. The skipper saw the ship and spun the wheel hard, trying to turn his boat toward the rampaging destroyer to fire his torpedoes from point-blank range—it was either that, or the Americans would be destroyed.

PT-109 couldn't turn fast enough.

It took just a single, terrifying instant for *Amagiri* to slice through the hull of *PT-109*. The skipper was almost crushed, at that moment thinking, *This is how it feels to be killed.* Two members of the 13-man crew died instantly. Two more were injured as *PT-109* exploded and burned. The two nearby American boats, *PT-162* and *PT-169*, knew a fatal blast when they saw one and

A PT boat similar to PT-109 *skims across the water. The boats were designed to travel at high speeds.* [© Corbis]

didn't wait around to search for survivors. They gunned their engines and raced into the night, fearful that other Japanese warships were in the vicinity. *Amagiri* didn't stop either, but sped on to Rabaul, even as the crew watched the small American craft burn in their wake.

The men of *PT-109* were on their own. Kennedy had to find a way to get his men to safety.

Later in life, when asked how that night helped him become a leader, he would shrug and say, "It was involuntary. They sank my boat." But the sinking of *PT-109* would be the making of John F. Kennedy—not because of what had just happened, but because of what happened next.

The back end of *PT-109* was already on its way to the bottom of the ocean. The forward section of the hull remained afloat because it had watertight compartments. Kennedy gathered the surviving crew members on this section to await help. But as morning turned to noon and what was left of *PT-109* sank lower and lower into the water, remaining with the wreckage meant either certain capture by Japanese troops or death by shark attack.

John Kennedy made a plan.

"We'll swim," he ordered the men, pointing to a cluster of green islands three miles to the southeast. He explained that these specks of land might be distant, but they were less likely than the closer islands to be inhabited by Japanese soldiers.

The men hung on to a piece of timber, using it as a flotation device as they kicked their way to the distant islands. Kennedy, who'd been a member of the swim team at Harvard College, towed a

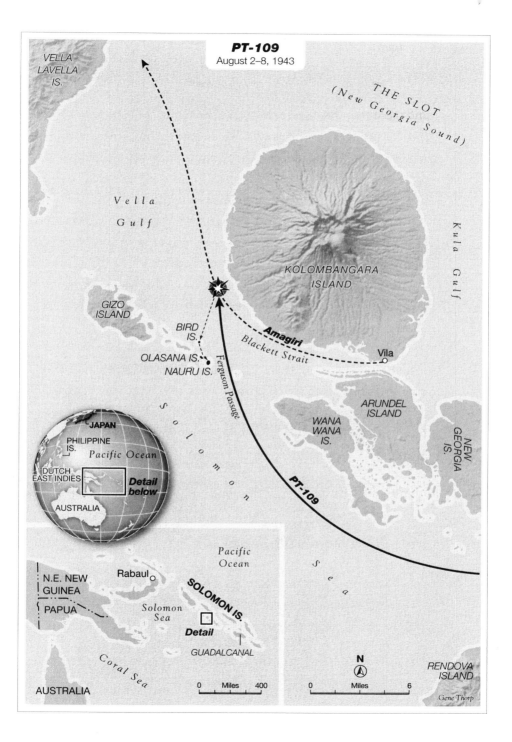

PT-109
August 2–8, 1943

VELLA
LAVELLA
IS.

THE SLOT
(New Georgia Sound)

V e l l a

G u l f

KOLOMBANGARA
ISLAND

K u l a

G u l f

GIZO
ISLAND

*BIRD
IS.*

Amagiri

Blackett Strait

Vila

OLASANA IS.
NAURU IS.

Ferguson Passage

ARUNDEL
ISLAND

WANA
WANA
IS.

NEW
GEORGIA
IS.

S
o
l
o
m
o
n

JAPAN

PHILIPPINE
IS.

Pacific Ocean

DUTCH
EAST INDIES

**Detail
below**

AUSTRALIA

PT-109

*Pacific
Ocean*

N.E. NEW
GUINEA

Rabaul

PAPUA

SOLOMON IS.

*Solomon
Sea*

Detail

S

e

a

GUADALCANAL

Coral Sea

AUSTRALIA

0   Miles   400

N

0   Miles   6

*RENDOVA
ISLAND*

Gene Thorp

badly burned crew member by placing a strap from the man's life jacket between his own teeth and pulling him. It took five hours for them to reach the island, which was not much: sand and a few palm trees surrounded by a razor-sharp coral reef. From one side to the other, it was just 100 yards. But it was land. After more than 15 hours in the ocean, there was no better place to be.

They hid in the shallows as a Japanese barge passed within a few hundred yards, and then they took shelter under low-hanging trees. Addressing his men, Kennedy outlined a plan: He would get back in that water and swim to a nearby island, which was close to the Ferguson Passage, a popular route for American PT boats. He would use a lantern to signal any he saw. If Kennedy made contact, he would signal to his crew with the lantern.

Although light-headed from dehydration and lack of food, Kennedy started out. When he reached the island, he couldn't find a sandy beach to crawl onto. His shoes scraped against the reef, which seemed endless. The coral sliced his hands and legs. So he decided on a courageous and foolhardy alternate course of action: He swam out into open water, lantern held aloft, hoping to signal a passing PT boat.

But on this night the U.S. Navy did not send PT boats through the Ferguson Passage. Kennedy treaded water in the blackness, waiting in vain for the sound of muffled propellers.

He finally gave up. But when he tried swimming back to his men, the currents worked against him. He was swept far out into the Blackett Strait and frantically lit the lamp to signal his men as he drifted past. On their island, his crew argued among themselves about whether the light they were seeing was real or an illusion brought on by hunger and thirst.

Carried by the currents, Kennedy floated all night long. The skin on his fingers wrinkled, and his body grew cold. But he never let go of the lamp.

As the sun came up, Kennedy was stunned to realize that the same currents that had pulled him out to sea had spun around and deposited him right where he started. He swam back safely to his

Kennedy and his men could see bombers like this B-17 in the air over the island. Gizo Island is below. [© Corbis]

men. After hours as a beacon in the darkness, the lamp finally went out once and for all.

Days passed. Kennedy and his men survived by choking down live snails and licking moisture off leaves. Sometimes they saw aircraft dogfighting in the skies, but they never spotted a rescue plane. They didn't know it, of course, but, even as they struggled to survive, their PT brethren held a memorial service in their honor.

After four days, Kennedy persuaded George Ross to attempt a swim with him. This time they headed for an island named Naru, where it was very possible they would run into Japanese soldiers. At this point in their ordeal, racked by hunger and excruciating thirst, they preferred capture to certain death.

The swim lasted an hour. At Naru, they came upon an abandoned enemy barge and saw two men hurriedly paddling away in a canoe. Kennedy was sure they were enemy soldiers. Kennedy and Ross searched the barge for supplies and found water and hardtack, very dry thick crackers. They also discovered a one-man canoe. After spending the day in hiding, Kennedy left Ross on Naru and paddled the small canoe back to his men.

Finally, Kennedy received a bit of good news. The men he had thought were Japanese soldiers were actually local islanders. He would discover that many Solomon Islanders worked as scouts for the Allies during the war. They had spotted Kennedy and Ross, and then paddled to *PT-109*'s crew to warn them about Japanese forces in the area.

Kennedy met these islanders in person the next morning when his canoe sank on the way back to Naru. These highly experienced men of the sea came out of nowhere to pluck him from the Pacific

This model of PT-109 *is on display in the White House.*
[JFK Presidential Library and Museum]

George "Barney" Ross (top) and John F. Kennedy (middle) were on PT-109 *when it was destroyed. Jim Reed (left) and Paul Fay (right) also served in the Solomon Islands. Photo taken in 1943.* [© Corbis]

and paddle him safely to George Ross. Before the islanders left, Kennedy carved a note into the shell of a fallen coconut:

NAURO ISL . . . COMMANDER

NATIVE KNOWS POS'IT . . .

HE CAN PILOT . . . 11 ALIVE . . . NEED SMALL BOAT . . .

KENNEDY

With that cryptic message in their possession, the natives paddled away.

Night fell. Rain poured down. Kennedy and Ross slept under a bush. Their arms and legs were swollen from bug bites and reef scratches.

As if in a mirage, Kennedy woke up to see four islanders standing over him. The sun was rising. Ross's limbs were horribly disfigured from his coral wounds; one arm had puffed up to the size of a football. Kennedy's own body was beginning to suffer from infection.

"I have a letter for you, sir," one of the men said in English.

An amazed Kennedy sat up and read the note. The scouts had taken his coconut to a New Zealand infantry detachment hidden nearby. The note was from the officer in charge. It said Kennedy should allow the islanders to paddle him to safety.

So it was that John F. Kennedy was placed in the bottom of a canoe, covered in palm fronds to hide him from Japanese aircraft, and paddled to a hidden location on New Georgia Island. When the canoe arrived at the water's edge, a young New Zealander stepped from the jungle. Kennedy came out from his hiding place and climbed out of the canoe.

"How do you do?" the New Zealander asked formally. "I'm Lieutenant Wincote." He pronounced his rank the British way: LEFFtenant.

"Hello. I'm Kennedy." The two men shook hands.

Wincote nodded toward the jungle. "Come up to my tent and have a cup of tea."

Kennedy and his men were soon rescued by the U.S. Navy and the six-day saga of *PT-109* came to an end. Kennedy was sent home to recuperate. His back, which had been painful for many years, was worse after the long days at sea. And he had malaria, which caused him to lose weight. Less than a year later, still thin but much healthier, John Kennedy was awarded the Navy and Marine Corps Medal and a citation for "extremely heroic conduct."

Newspapers carried stories about the brave young man's adventure. The story of *PT-109* became a legend, and John Kennedy came to be known as a hero. Soon the story would help him become a politician and lead him to the presidency.

CHAPTER FOUR

AUGUST 12, 1944
Over the English Channel

THERE IS ANOTHER EVENT that jump-starts John Kennedy's journey to the Oval Office. Kennedy's older brother, Joe, is not as lucky as John at cheating death. Joe is a U.S. Navy bomber pilot flying antisubmarine missions against the Nazis in Europe. His experimental Liberator bomber plane is carrying 21,000 pounds of the explosive TNT when it detonates over the English Channel on August 12, 1944. There is no body to bury and no memento of the tragedy to place on JFK's desk.

Joe was the firstborn son. His father expected him to be a politician. John is next in line. Because he is the second-born in a family where great things are expected from the oldest son,

A B-29 Liberator bomber. Joe Kennedy was flying a version of this aircraft on its first mission when it exploded. [Eugene Berman/Shutterstock.com]

John has not had a very hard life. He was a sickly child, grew into a young man fond of books and parties, and, with the exception of commanding *PT-109*, has shown no interest in pursuing a leadership position. He thought he'd be a writer or a reporter.

Growing up, John looked up to his charismatic older brother, but he took his orders from his father. Joseph P. Kennedy is one of the wealthiest and

Joseph Kennedy Jr. in Switzerland in 1939.
[JFK Presidential Library and Museum]

Joseph Kennedy Sr.; his wife, Rose; and eight of their children at their summer home in Hyannis Port, Massachusetts, in 1931. From left to right: Bobby, Jack, Eunice, Jean, Joseph Senior, Rose with Pat in front of her, Kathleen, Joe Junior, and Rosemary. Edward was not yet born. [JFK Presidential Library and Museum]

most powerful men in America and a former ambassador to Great Britain.

All nine Kennedy children obey the patriarch. John Kennedy will one day liken the relationship to that of puppets and their puppet master. Joseph P. Kennedy decides how his children will spend their lives and monitors their every action.

Young Joe's tragic death marks the moment when John F. Kennedy inherits the role of politician in the Kennedy family.

Joseph Kennedy Sr. with his two oldest sons, Joe Jr. and John, in Florida in 1931. [JFK Presidential Library and Museum]

CHAPTER FIVE

1945–1946
Chicago, Illinois, and Boston, Massachusetts

THE LONG WAR FINALLY ENDS. Nazi Germany surrenders on May 7, and Japan surrenders on August 14. Soldiers and sailors return home with high hopes. The American economy is strong, so men and women can find jobs and buy homes. John Kennedy is working in Chicago as a reporter writing about the founding of the United Nations and even traveling to Britain to report on elections there. But he hears from his father almost every day. And his father wants him to run for office.

1946

So, less than six months after the war ends, John Fitzgerald Kennedy is one of 10 candidates running in the Democratic

Next page: *The day after the surrender of Germany was declared V-E day (Victory in Europe day). It is still celebrated in some countries.* [© Bettmann/Corbis]

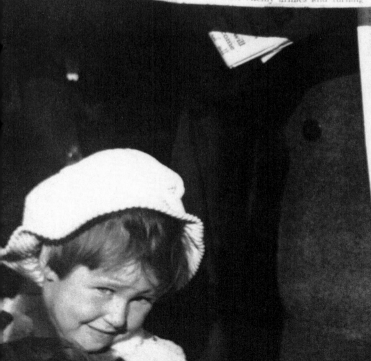

Schoolchildren in Chicago celebrate V-E day. [© Corbis]

primary of Boston's Eleventh Congressional District. Veteran politicians in Boston don't give him a chance of winning. But JFK doesn't mind being the underdog. He recruits a well-connected fellow World War II veteran named Dave Powers to help run his campaign. Powers, a rising political star in his own right, is at first reluctant to help the skinny young man who introduces himself by saying, "My name is Jack Kennedy. I'm a candidate for Congress."

Dave Powers was with Kennedy during all his campaigns. He heard Kennedy's first speech in Boston in 1946 and his last in Fort Worth in 1963. [© Bettmann/Corbis]

But Powers watches in awe as Kennedy stands before a packed hall on a cold Saturday night in January 1946 and gives a dazzling campaign speech. The occasion is a meeting of Gold Star Mothers, women who have lost sons in World War II. Kennedy speaks for only 10 minutes, telling the assembled ladies why he is running for office. The audience cannot see that his hands shake anxiously. But they hear his well-chosen words as he reminds them of his own war record and explains why their sons'

MORE JOBS · MORE HOUSING · MORE INDUSTRY
JOHN F. **KENNEDY**
For CONGRESS · 11TH DISTRICT · PRIMARIES TUES. JUNE 18

sacrifices were so meaningful, speaking in an honest, sincere voice about their bravery.

Then Kennedy pauses before softly referring to his fallen brother, Joe: "I think I know how all you mothers feel. You see, my mother is a Gold Star Mother, too."

Women surge toward him when the speech concludes. Tears in their eyes, they reach out to touch this young man who reminds them of the sons they lost, telling him that he has their support. In that instant, Dave Powers is convinced; he goes to work for Kennedy right then and there. It is Dave Powers who seizes on *PT-109* as a vital aspect of the campaign, mailing voters a reprint of a story about the August nights in 1943 that show the selfless bravery of a wealthy young man for whom some might otherwise not be inclined to vote.

Thanks to Dave Powers's insistence on making the most of the *PT-109* story, John F. Kennedy is elected to Congress on November 5, 1946.

Kennedy's campaign slogan was "More jobs, more housing, more industry." [© Corbis]

THE MAKING OF
A LEADER

The White House swimming pool was built for President Franklin Roosevelt. The press briefing room was constructed over it in 1970. [JFK Presidential Library and Museum]

CHAPTER SIX

FEBRUARY 1961
The White House 1:00 P.M.

THE PRESIDENT OF THE UNITED STATES is on schedule. Almost every afternoon, at precisely 1:00 P.M., he slips into the heated indoor pool located between the White House and the West Wing. John Kennedy does this to soothe his aching back. The pain is constant and so bad that he often uses crutches or a cane to get around, though rarely in public. He wears a back brace, sleeps on an extra-firm mattress, and receives regular injections of an anesthetic to ease his suffering. Aides know to look for a tightening of his jaw as a sign that the president's back is acting up. The half hour of breaststroke and the heat of the pool are part of Kennedy's physical therapy.

The White House staff is getting used to the new president and his family. Very little that was unexpected happened in the White House during the eight years the previous president, Dwight Eisenhower, lived there.

But now everything has changed. The Kennedys are much

less formal than the Eisenhowers. Receiving lines are being abolished, giving formal functions a more casual feel. The first lady is readying the East Room for performances by some of America's most notable musicians, such as cellist and composer Pablo Casals, opera singer Grace Bumbry, jazz artist Paul Winter, and even full symphony orchestras.

Still, the White House is a serious place. The president's daily schedule revolves around periods of intense work followed by breaks for swimming and family time. He wakes up each morning around seven and reads the newspapers in bed, including the *New York Times*, *Washington Post*, and *Wall Street Journal*. Kennedy is a speed-reader; he can read and understand 1,200 words per minute. He is done with the newspapers in just 15 minutes, and then moves on to a pile of briefing books, reports prepared by his staff that summarize information about events going on around the world.

The president then has his usual breakfast in bed: orange juice, bacon, toast slathered in marmalade, two soft-boiled eggs, and coffee with cream.

He is in the Oval Office at nine o'clock sharp. He sits back in his chair and listens as his appointments secretary, Kenny O'Donnell, maps out his

Kenny O'Donnell was Robert Kennedy's roommate at Harvard College. The two were also on the football team. This portrait was taken in 1961.
[JFK Presidential Library and Museum]

Evelyn Lincoln was Kennedy's personal secretary from his days in the Senate until his death. Caroline visited her office in the White House almost daily. [© Bettmann/Corbis]

schedule. Throughout the morning, as Kennedy takes calls and listens to advisers brief him on what is happening in the rest of the world, he is interrupted by his handpicked staff. In addition to Dave Powers, who is now special assistant to the president, and

Sometimes business turns into pleasure, as when Kennedy and prime minister of Ireland Sean Lemass (in front of the flag) try out golf clubs.
[JFK Presidential Library and Museum]

Kenny O'Donnell, there are also the former Harvard history professor Arthur Schlesinger Jr.; Ted Sorensen, the Nebraska-born special counselor and adviser; and Pierre Salinger, the former child prodigy pianist who serves as press secretary.

After swimming, Kennedy eats a quick lunch upstairs in the first family's private rooms, often referred to as "the residence." He then naps for exactly 45 minutes. Other great figures in history such as Winston Churchill napped during the day. For Kennedy, it is a means of rejuvenation.

Then it's back to the Oval Office, most nights working as late as 8:00 P.M. After business hours, Kennedy often puts two feet up on his desk and casually tosses ideas back and forth with his staff. It is the president's favorite time of the day.

When everyone has cleared out, he makes his way back upstairs to the residence for his evening meal with his family or with friends Jackie invites.

CHAPTER SEVEN

WINTER 1961

United States, Cuba, and Soviet Union

THE WORLD OUTSIDE THE **WHITE HOUSE** is turbulent. The Cold War is raging. Americans are terrified of the Soviet Union and its arsenal of nuclear weapons. Towns stock bomb shelters, and in schools, children practice curling up under their desks to protect themselves in case of attack. J. Edgar Hoover and the FBI have created an atmosphere of suspicion by telling people that Communists are threatening America.

Ninety miles south of Florida, Fidel Castro has recently taken over Cuba. Castro is also a young, vibrant leader, and he inspires

These children are arranging cans in a bomb shelter. [© Seattle Post-Intelligencer Collection; Museum of History and Industy/Corbis]

Fidel Castro toured the United States for eleven days in 1959, three months after his revolutionaries overthrew the Cuban dictator. Here he arrives in Washington, D.C., to meet with Vice President Nixon.
[LOC, DIG-ppmsc-03256]

Cubans much as John Kennedy inspires Americans. But Castro is a friend of the Soviets and communism, not of the United States and democracy.

In America's Southern states, there is growing racial strife. Since 1957, Martin Luther King Jr. has been an inspirational leader in the civil rights movement. His commitment to nonviolent protest has inspired sit-ins and marches throughout the South. Protesters insist on equal treatment under the law for all people, regardless of the color of their skin. In the spring and summer of 1961, college students from around the country travel to the South by bus. White and black kids sit together to see if the police or security people will make them separate, because at the time, bus travel between states is segregated. These brave people are called "freedom riders."

Freedom riders on their way from New York City to Washington, D.C., to picket the White House in support of equal rights for all people. [© Bettmann/Corbis]

On August 13, the border between communist East Berlin and democratic West Berlin is closed to keep people from deserting the East by running across the border to the West. The Communists build a massive concrete wall to encircle West Berlin and shoot anyone who tries to crawl over it.

Inside the White House, Jackie Kennedy is getting used to her role as first lady. Like her husband, Jackie was raised with wealth. She attended expensive girls' boarding schools and Vassar College, and spent her junior year in Paris. Upon Jackie's return to the United States, she transferred to George Washington University, in Washington, D.C., receiving a diploma in 1951.

The Kennedy family arrives back from a vacation in Palm Beach, Florida, where JFK's parents have a home. [JFK Presidential Library and Museum]

JFK, Jackie, LBJ, and Lady Bird at a diplomatic reception in 1962.
[JFK Presidential Library and Museum]

Growing up, the first lady was taught to be extremely private and to hold thoughts deep within herself. She likes to maintain "a certain quality of mystery about her," a friend will later say. The American people respond to her and to the little bit of mystery that surrounds her, as well as to her glamorous hairdos and clothes.

Jackie Kennedy likes to think of herself as a traditional wife,

John Jr. exploring under his father's desk. [© Bettmann/Corbis]

focusing most of her attention on her husband and children. But she also has a major project—an extensive renovation of the White House. The current style of furniture, rugs, and curtains is from the early 1950s, when Harry Truman was president. Many pieces of furniture are copies instead of period originals. Jackie wants the White House to look like it did when it was first built. She has arranged for the White House to be declared a museum in order to preserve it for all Americans.

She thinks she has years to finish the renovation.

At least four. Perhaps even eight if her husband is reelected.

March 17, 1961

In the far-off city of Minsk in the Soviet Union, Lee Harvey Oswald has just met a woman at a dance for union workers. The 19-year-old beauty wears a red dress and white shoes and styles her hair in what he believes to be the French fashion. Marina Prusakova is reluctant to smile because of her bad teeth, but the two dance, and he walks her home. Later, he writes in his journal, "We like each other right away."

Between the nights of March 18 and March 30, they spend a great deal of time together. "We walk," he writes. "I talk a little about myself, she talks a lot about herself."

Their relationship takes a sudden turn on March 30, when Oswald enters the hospital for an adenoid operation. Marina visits him constantly, and by the time Lee is discharged, he knows he "must have her." On April 30, they are married. Marina almost immediately becomes pregnant.

Very quickly, life is complicated for Lee Harvey Oswald. The former bachelor now has two people to provide for, and he has to figure out if he can take a Soviet citizen with him back to the United States.

This marriage is important to Oswald. It makes him feel adult and in charge. But he doesn't really know what a good marriage is. Oswald hasn't seen one close up in

This photograph of Marina Oswald was in Lee Harvey Oswald's wallet when he was arrested. [© Corbis]

Young Lee at a zoo in New York. [© Corbis]

his life. His father dies before he is born and his mother sends him to an orphanage when he is four years old. When she finally takes him back for good, he is twelve. They move from New Orleans to New York City, where Marguerite Oswald works all day in a dress shop. Lee drifts around the city, traveling by subway, when he should be in school.

One day he picks up a flyer about two people who are about to be executed for spying for Russia. Oswald writes in his diary: "I was looking for a key to my environment, and then I discovered socialist literature. I had to dig for my books in the back dusty shelves of libraries."

Oswald never finishes school. He joins the Marines when he is seventeen and is trained in marksmanship. But he can't seem to fit in. He is court-martialed twice, once for having an illegal pistol and once for attacking a sergeant. Very soon, he is learning Russian and making plans to defect to the Soviet Union. He lasted three years in the Marines and has been in the Soviet Union for two. It seems that Lee Harvey Oswald hasn't found a place to belong.

CHAPTER EIGHT

APRIL 17, 1961

Washington, D.C./Bay of Pigs, Cuba 9:40 A.M.

JOHN F. KENNEDY ABSENTMINDEDLY buttons his suit coat. He is seated aboard *Marine One*, his presidential Marine Corps helicopter, as it lands on the South Lawn of the White House. He has just spent a most unrelaxing weekend at Glen Ora, the family's rented country retreat in Virginia.

Kennedy is preoccupied with Cuba. A battlefield is taking shape there. Kennedy has authorized a secret invasion of the island nation, sending 1,400 anti-Castro exiles to do a job that the U.S. military, by rule of international law, cannot do itself. The freedom fighters' goal is nothing less than the overthrow of the Cuban government. The plan has been in the works since long before Kennedy was elected. Both the Central Intelligence Agency and the Joint Chiefs of Staff representing the Army, Navy, Air Force, and Marines have assured the president that the mission will succeed. But it is Kennedy who has given the go-ahead, and it is he who will take the blame if the mission fails.

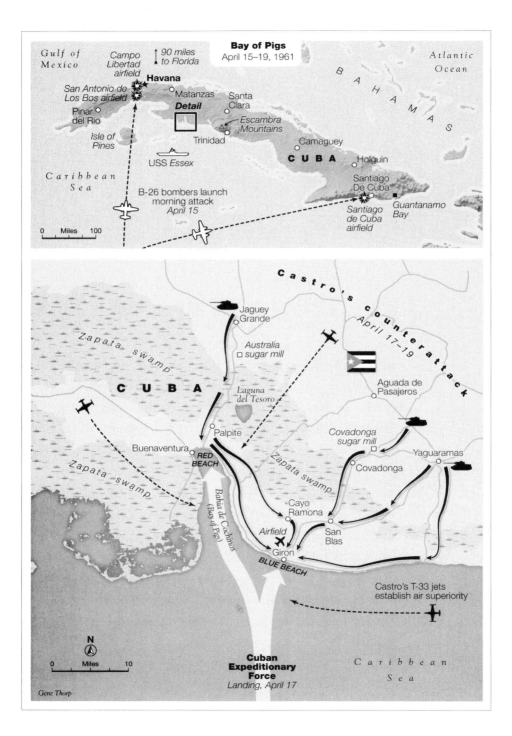

Bay of Pigs
April 15–19, 1961

Gulf of Mexico

↑ 90 miles to Florida

Campo Libertad airfield

Havana

San Antonio de Los Bos airfield

Pinar del Rio

Matanzas

Santa Clara

Detail

Escambra Mountains

Trinidad

Isle of Pines

USS *Essex*

Caribbean Sea

B-26 bombers launch morning attack April 15

Atlantic Ocean

BAHAMAS

Camaguey

Holguin

CUBA

Santiago De Cuba

Santiago de Cuba airfield

Guantanamo Bay

0 Miles 100

Castro's counterattack April 17–19

Jaguey Grande

Zapata swamp

Australia □ sugar mill

CUBA

Laguna del Tesoro

Palpite

Buenaventura

RED BEACH

Zapata swamp

Zapata swamp

Aguada de Pasajeros

Covadonga sugar mill

Covadonga

Yaguaramas

Cayo Ramona

Airfield

San Blas

Giron

BLUE BEACH

Bahía de Cochinos (Bay of Pigs)

Castro's T-33 jets establish air superiority

N

0 Miles 10

Cuban Expeditionary Force
Landing, April 17

Caribbean Sea

Gene Thorp

In the days leading up to the scheduled invasion, President Kennedy reviewed the CIA's plan. He wanted the invasion to seem as if it had been generated solely by Cuban exiles, thereby masking American government involvement. This required an out-of-the-way landing area where men and supplies could go ashore quietly, then slip into the countryside unnoticed.

The CIA suggested a location, known as Bahía de Cochinos—loosely translated as the "Bay of Pigs." The landing would take place at night.

On April 14, just two days after giving a press conference in which he promised there would be no intervention by U.S. forces in Cuba, Kennedy gave Operation Zapata, as the Bay of Pigs invasion was known, the official go-ahead.

April 14 was a Friday. After launching the invasion, there was nothing for the president to do but wait. So he flew to Glen Ora to be with Jackie and the kids, where he endured a gut-wrenching weekend waiting for news from Cuba. When word finally came, almost none of it was good.

It started on Saturday morning, when eight B-26 bombers piloted by Cuban freedom fighters attacked three Cuban air bases. The bombings barely damaged the Cuban air force. But Fidel Castro was furious. He immediately accused the United States of involvement in the attack.

Things only got worse after that. A diversionary landing on Saturday was supposed to put about 160 anti-Castro Cuban freedom fighters ashore near Guantánamo Bay, but it was canceled

This photo, printed in a Cuban newspaper, shows the Cuban army attacking the U.S.-backed freedom fighters. [© Bettmann/Corbis]

when a crucial boat broke down. In a separate incident, Cuban forces arrested a small band of freedom fighters who were already on the island.

By Saturday afternoon, the Cuban ambassador to the United Nations was addressing the General Assembly, denouncing the

United States for its attack—in response to which Adlai Stevenson, the U.S. ambassador, repeated JFK's promise that no American forces would ever wage war in Cuba.

In the dead of night, just after Sunday turned to Monday, the landing force of 1,400 Cuban exiles from Brigade 2506 powered toward the Bay of Pigs aboard a small fleet of freighters and landing vessels. Their hopes were high—their dream was to regain control of their homeland.

John Kennedy stands in the Oval Office, helpless to stop what he has started. At his side is his brother Bobby, his closest friend and adviser.

The news from the landing beaches is not good: The freedom fighters have failed to secure key roads and other strategic points. There is no way off the beach for the men of Brigade 2506. Cuban forces have pinned them down. The invasion is stalled.

A distraught JFK shares his fears with Bobby. The president knows when speaking with his brother that he is safe from security leaks or attempts to undermine his authority. But even now, with Bobby at his side, John Kennedy feels the crushing loneliness of being the president of the United States. He has made this mess in Cuba. If only he can find a way to turn this disaster into a victory.

But that is not to be.

April 19, 1961

In a last-ditch attempt to salvage the invasion, the president reluctantly authorizes one hour of air cover starting at 6:30 A.M., to be provided by six unmarked jets from the Navy aircraft carrier *Essex*. The jets are to rendezvous with the B-26 bombers piloted by Cuban freedom fighters and keep the Cuban aircraft at bay.

Now there is more bad news: incredibly, the CIA and the Pentagon didn't account for the time zone difference between Cuba and the freedom fighters' air base in Nicaragua. Jets from the *Essex* and the B-26 bombers from Nicaragua arrive at the rendezvous one hour apart. The two groups of aircraft never meet up. As a result,

Robert Kennedy was his brother's closest friend and confidant. Here they stand outside the door leading to the Oval Office. [JFK Presidential Library and Museum]

several B-26s and their pilots are shot down by the Cuban air force. Pierre Salinger, the president's press secretary, discovers Kennedy alone in the White House residence, weeping after hearing the news.

By 5:30 P.M. on the night of April 19, Cuban forces have taken complete control of the Bay of Pigs. The invasion is over.

In addition to the dead and captured on the ground, Castro's forces have sunk almost a dozen invasion vessels, including those carrying food and ammunition, and shot down nine B-26 bombers.

The defeat is a major humiliation for the United States. Kennedy is forced to give a press conference and take full blame. "There's an old saying that victory has a hundred fathers and defeat is an orphan. . . ." What matters, he says, is that "I am the responsible officer of the government."

Amazingly, Kennedy's approval rises to 83 percent after the invasion, proving to the president that the American people stand firmly behind his actions against Castro. The rating temporarily makes him one of the most popular presidents of the 20th century.

Meanwhile, in the Soviet Union, the U.S. State Department has decided to return Lee Harvey Oswald's American passport to him and allow him to return home. He delays his departure until Marina and their unborn child can travel with him.

He also puts off telling Marina that they are going anywhere.

At last, Oswald breaks the news. "My wife is slightly startled," he writes in his journal in June, after finally telling Marina that they are leaving the Soviet Union, most likely forever, "but then encourages me to do what I wish to do."

Marina is on the verge of leaving behind everything she knows for a life of uncertainty with a man she barely knows. But she accepts this hard reality because she has already learned one important thing about Lee Harvey Oswald: He always does what he wants to do, no matter how many obstacles are thrown in his path.

Always.

[© Corbis]

CHAPTER NINE

FEBRUARY 14, 1962

Washington, D.C. 8:00 P.M. EST on NBC and CBS TV

THE FIRST LADY GLIDES ALONE down a hallway, walking straight toward the television cameras. Her outfit and lipstick are a striking red, but the camera will broadcast only in black and white, so this detail is lost on the 46 million Americans tuning in to watch her televised tour of the White House. This is Jackie's moment in the national spotlight, a chance to show off her ongoing effort to restore the historic building.

She begins by narrating a brief history of the White House. Viewers hear her voice as images of historical drawings and photographs fill the screen. "Piece by piece," she says, "the interior of the president's house was put back together."

The first lady once again steps before the camera to take viewers on a walk around her new home, now followed by the show's host, Charles Collingwood of CBS. Jackie's personal touches are everywhere, from the new draperies, whose designs she sketched herself, to the new guidebook she authorized to raise funds for the restoration. She has scoured White House storage rooms and the National Gallery of Art, turning up assorted treasures such as paintings by Paul Cézanne, Teddy Roosevelt's drinking mugs, and James Monroe's gold French flatware. President Kennedy's new desk was another of Jackie's finds. The *Resolute* desk, as it is known, was carved from the timbers of an ill-fated British vessel and was a gift from Queen Victoria to President Rutherford B. Hayes in 1880. Jackie found it in the White House broadcast room, buried beneath a pile of electronics. She promptly had it relocated to the Oval Office.

"Thank you, Mr. President," concludes reporter Charles Collingwood. "And thank you, Mrs. Kennedy, for showing us this wonderful house in which you live, and all of the wonderful things you're bringing to it."

John Kennedy has joined his wife on camera for the last few minutes of the broadcast special, explaining the importance of Jackie's ongoing efforts and what the White House means as a symbol of America.

Jackie's White House tour is one of the most watched shows in the history of television. In fact, it earns the first lady a special Emmy Award. America is now smitten. Jacqueline Kennedy is a superstar.

The first lady escorts the country through the newly refurbished White House. She won an Emmy Award for this televised tour. Here she is showing the State Dining Room. [© Associated Press]

CHAPTER TEN

EARLY 1962
Minsk

IN MINSK, THE OSWALDS' DAUGHTER IS BORN. Lee Harvey Oswald is ready to return home. The plan is for him, Marina, and baby June Lee to take the train to the American embassy in Moscow to pick up their travel documents. The Oswalds arrive in Moscow on May 24, 1962.

On June 1, they board a train from Moscow to the Netherlands. Lee Oswald carries a promissory note from the U.S. embassy for $435.71 to help start his life in America. They board the SS *Maasdam*, bound for America, and stay belowdecks most of the journey. Oswald is ashamed of Marina's cheap dresses and doesn't want her to be seen in public. He passes the time in their small cabin writing about his growing disillusionment with governmental power.

The *Maasdam* docks in Hoboken, New Jersey, on June 13, 1962. The Oswalds pass through customs without incident and take a small room at a New York City Times Square hotel.

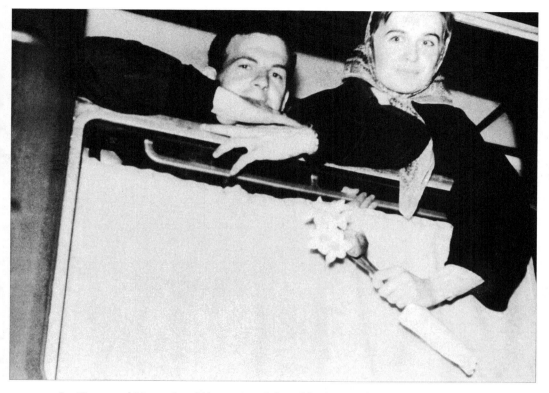

Lee Harvey and Marina Oswald leaving Minsk, bound for the United States. [© Corbis]

Thanks to a loan from his brother, Robert, Lee Harvey Oswald and his family fly to Dallas. The city is simmering with a rage that mirrors Oswald's ongoing personal unhappiness in many ways. The South swung in President Kennedy's favor during the election, but there are pockets of militant anger; people grumble about Kennedy being the first Roman Catholic president and his desire to bring about racial equality.

This is the environment into which the Oswald family arrives.

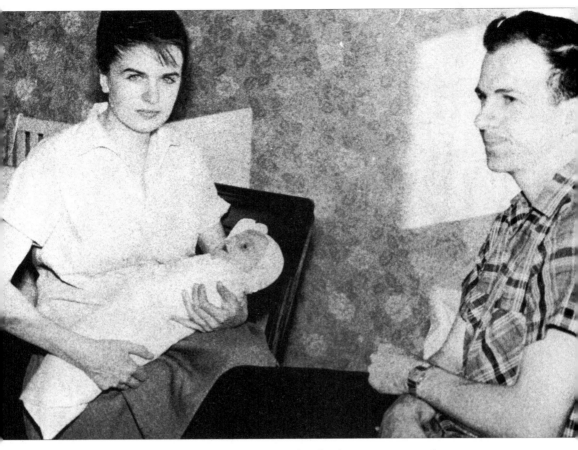

Marina and Lee Harvey Oswald with their daughter, June Lee, in 1962. [© Corbis]

They land at a Dallas-area airport called Love Field, where the president and first lady will touch down aboard *Air Force One* in 17 short months. Lee's brother takes them to his home in nearby Fort Worth.

Oswald is unhappy that his return to the United States has not attracted widespread media attention—or any media attention at all, for that matter. He thinks that he should have been noticed. But even as he fumes that the press is nowhere in sight, he is being watched—but secretly.

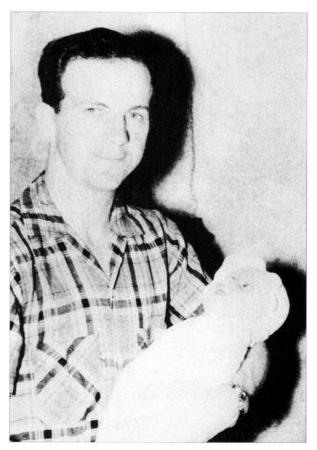

Lee Harvey Oswald holding baby June. [© Corbis]

CHAPTER ELEVEN

AUGUST 16, 1962
Fort Worth, Texas

IT IS BRUTALLY HOT IN FORT WORTH. FBI special agents John Fain and Arnold J. Brown have been waiting all day to see Lee Harvey Oswald. They sit in an unmarked car just down the street from Oswald's newly rented apartment. Fain and Brown work for J. Edgar Hoover, the head of the FBI. Hoover's intense preoccupation is finding and arresting anyone who sympathizes with Communists. He seems to suspect almost everybody and has created an atmosphere of suspicion and fear in thousands of innocent people.

The Oswald case is nothing new to Special Agent Fain. Back when Oswald first defected to the Soviet Union, Fain was assigned a minor investigation of Oswald's mother because she had mailed $25 to her son in the Soviet Union. The FBI was following even the smallest leads to find Communist sympathizers.

John Fain had also spoken face-to-face with Oswald just

seven weeks earlier, on June 26. Oswald's case has been designated an "internal security" investigation, based on the concern that his defection might make him a threat to national security. Fain's job is to find out whether the Russians trained Oswald to perform a job against the United States. Something about the first interview, which lasted two hours, didn't sit well with Fain. One question that Fain asked and Oswald never answered in a completely truthful manner was

J. Edgar Hoover, director of the Federal Bureau of Investigation of the United States. [LOC, DIG-ppmscc-03262]

whether the Russians demanded anything in return for letting him come back to America. A second question interests Fain: Why did Oswald go to the Soviet Union in the first place? Oswald didn't answer that one either. He danced around it, talking about "his own personal reasons," that "it was something that I did." Fain didn't like Oswald's attitude, thinking him proud and rude.

John Fain needs these questions answered. He's a very thorough man and takes it upon himself to interview Lee Harvey Oswald one more time.

At 5:30 P.M., the two agents see Oswald walking down the street. Fain drives up beside him. "Hi, Lee. How are you?" he says out the car window. "Would you mind talking with us for just a few minutes?"

The three men talk for a little over an hour. Oswald is friendlier than before, less defensive. He explains that he's been in touch with the Soviet embassy, but only because it is required for Soviet citizens such as Marina to inform the embassy of their location on a regular basis. When pressed about whether this involved discussions with Soviet intelligence officials, Oswald doesn't answer directly,

but wonders aloud why anyone would want to discuss spying with a guy like him. "He didn't feel like he was of any importance" to the Russians, Fain will later testify.

At 6:45 P.M., Oswald is released from the car and goes inside his home.

But Lee Harvey Oswald and the FBI will soon meet again.

Marina and Lee Harvey Oswald with their daughter, June Lee, in 1962. [© Corbis]

CHAPTER TWELVE

OCTOBER 16, 1962
The White House 8:45 A.M.

THE PRESIDENT OF THE UNITED STATES is rolling around on the bedroom floor with his children. The fitness expert Jack LaLanne is on the television telling JFK, Caroline, and John to touch their toes.

The president will soon get dressed. The kids will stick around and watch cartoons. Jackie might sit with him as he wraps his back brace into place before putting on his shirt. Sometimes during the day, John and Caroline walk into the Oval Office and play on the floor or even beneath

John Jr. visits his father on the porch outside the Oval Office. [JFK Presidential Library and Museum]

The president's children often visited the Oval Office. In this photograph, Caroline is four years old and John Jr. is 23 months old. [JFK Presidential Library and Museum]

the presidential desk. Jackie fiercely protects the children from the public eye. But the president takes a larger view, realizing that America is enthralled by such a young first family and wants to hear about their daily life. Caroline and John have become celebrities in their own right, although they don't know it. Photographers, writers, news magazines, and daily newspapers chronicling their young lives are just a fact of life.

Caroline on her pony, Macaroni, a gift to her from Vice President Johnson. Macaroni received fan mail from people around the country.
[JFK Presidential Library and Museum]

John, almost two years old, likes to stop at his father's secretary's typewriter on his way in to the Oval Office and pretend to type a letter. Caroline, who is nearly five years old, often brings one or more of the family's dogs when she pays a visit to her father. In fact, the Kennedy children have turned the White House into a menagerie, with dogs, hamsters, a cat, parakeets, and even a pony named Macaroni. JFK is allergic to dog hair, but he never lets on.

Caroline inspects a snowman built for her outside the White House. [JFK Presidential Library and Museum]

Kennedy, like every president since John Adams became the White House's first resident in 1800, has learned that life inside the White House is complicated. Mornings are the only time the president can be carefree, unrehearsed, and, best of all, unwatched by a curious public.

But on this Tuesday morning in October, a knock on the president's bedroom door intrudes on his private time with the children.

National Security Adviser McGeorge Bundy steps through the door.

Bundy has very bad news to deliver. He learned of it last night but intentionally waited until now to tell the president. John Kennedy was in New York to deliver a speech and didn't return to the White House until very late. The national security adviser wanted to make sure Kennedy had a full night of sleep before he received the news. Bundy knows that from now until the moment this problem is solved, the president will be lucky to get any rest. For what McGeorge Bundy is about to tell JFK could change the course of history.

"Mr. President," the 43-year-old Bundy calmly informs Kennedy, "there is now hard photographic evidence, which you will see later, that the Russians have offensive missiles in Cuba."

United States U-2 spy planes flying over Cuba have confirmed that six Soviet medium-range ballistic missile sites and 21 medium-range bomber planes are on that island, just 90 miles from the United States. Each of the airplanes is capable of launching nuclear weapons from

JFK with McGeorge Bundy, special assistant to the president for national security. [JFK Presidential Library and Museum]

thousands of feet in the air. The medium-range ballistic missiles could travel as far as Arkansas.

The nuclear bombs the planes and missiles carry could kill 80 million Americans in a matter of minutes. Millions more would die later from the radioactive fallout.

The president has dealt with crisis after crisis since taking office 21 months ago. But nothing—not the Bay of Pigs, not civil rights, not the Berlin Wall—can even remotely compare with this.

JFK orders McGeorge Bundy to immediately schedule a top-secret meeting of the national security staff. He then phones Bobby, telling him that "we have some big trouble. I want you over here." The president decides not to deviate from his normal schedule; he doesn't want the news about this "second Cuba" to get out quite yet. He has several good reasons for this. One is that he doesn't want to panic the American public. He needs to learn about the situation and make a plan for moving forward before talking to the press.

Another reason has to do with JFK's political best interests. The president long ago assured the American public that he would not allow the Soviets to install offensive weapons in Cuba. Now Nikita

One of many conversations during the Cuban missile crisis. Here, Kennedy talks with Maxwell D. Taylor, chairman of the Joint Chiefs of Staff, and Robert S. McNamara, secretary of defense. [JFK Presidential Library and Museum]

Labeled U.S. spy plane photo of launch sites being prepared in Cuba. [© Bettmann/Corbis]

Khrushchev, the premier of the Soviet Union, is calling Kennedy's bluff.

The final, and by far the most important, reason the president doesn't want word leaking out about the missiles in Cuba is that he does not want the Russian leadership to know that he is on to their secret.

So on the morning of October 16, Kennedy leaves the residence and walks down to the Oval Office to start his day.

Two hours later, the top-secret meeting to talk about the Soviet missiles begins. Kennedy takes a seat at the center of the table, not the head. Bobby sits across from him, as does LBJ. Eleven other men are in attendance, all handpicked for their expertise and loyalty to the president.

Photos taken by U-2 spy planes show that the Soviet missiles are being prepared for launch. Experts think that the nuclear warheads, the bombs that the missiles and planes will carry, are on Soviet ships heading for Cuba. So the main objective is to prevent these ships from reaching Cuba and unloading the bombs. The

The ExComm group meets to discuss the situation in Cuba.
[JFK Presidential Library and Museum]

JFK, in his rocking chair, meets with Soviet foreign minister Andrei Gromyko, on Kennedy's right, on October 18, 1962. The Soviet ambassador to the U.S. is on Gromyko's right. White House Secret Service agent Frank Yeager stands behind the photographers. [JFK Presidential Library and Museum]

group presents various military opinions. The first is a limited air strike. The second is a broader air strike, on a broader number of targets. The third is a naval blockade of Cuban waters to keep the Soviet ships away.

Bobby, who has listened quietly throughout the 70-minute meeting, finally speaks up, suggesting that a full-scale invasion of Cuba might be necessary. It is the only way to prevent Russian bombs from ever being placed on Cuban soil.

Even as military force seems like the only solution, JFK is still troubled by the question of motive. Why is Nikita Khrushchev trying to provoke the Americans into war?

The president doesn't know the answer. But two things are apparent: Those missiles must be removed and, far more important, those nuclear warheads cannot be allowed to reach Cuba.

Ever.

On October 18, Kennedy meets privately with Soviet foreign minister Andrei Gromyko. It is Gromyko who requests the meeting, not knowing that the Americans have discovered that the Soviets have placed offensive missiles in Cuba. The topics of discussion are the goings-on in Berlin and Soviet leader Khrushchev's upcoming visit to America. Kennedy skillfully guides the subject toward the topic of nuclear weapons. Gromyko then lies to the president's face, stating most adamantly that the Soviet Union would never become involved in the furnishing of *offensive* weapons to Cuba. He says that the Soviet advisers in Cuba are training the Cuban military to use *defensive* weapons.

Of course, Kennedy knows that Gromyko is lying.

An SS-4 missile, the kind the Soviets sent to Cuba.
[© Shutterstock.com]

CHAPTER THIRTEEN

OCTOBER 19 TO 25, 1962
The White House

THERE IS NO DAY AND THERE IS NO NIGHT in the Kennedy White House as the Cuban confrontation escalates. The president is in such pain from his back that he gets around on crutches, further adding to the tension.

For two days, Kennedy and his close advisers debate the top-secret threat to the United States. Photos taken by U-2 spy planes show that people are working around the clock to complete the missile sites, meaning that warheads could be launched toward the United States within a matter of days. No one leaks this information to the press. Not even the Congress is told.

On the night of Monday, October 22, at 7:00 P.M., the scene changes. President John Fitzgerald Kennedy appears on national television to inform America about the potentially lethal missiles in Cuba—and what he plans to do about them.

Next page: *Cameramen film President Kennedy's address to the nation, October 22, 1962, outlining his strategy for the removal of Soviet nuclear warheads in Cuba.*
[JFK Presidential Library and Museum]

On October 22, 1962, customers in an electronics store watch President Kennedy's address to the nation about the Cuban missile crisis. [© Ralph Crane/Getty]

"Good evening, my fellow citizens," he says in greeting from his study at the White House. There are deep grooves under his greenish-gray eyes, giving him a haggard look instead of the vibrant, youthful countenance the nation is used to seeing.

This broadcast from the White House is quite the opposite of Jackie's lighthearted tour eight months earlier. Kennedy must make the most powerful speech of his life. He does not smile. His face is stern. There is menace in his eyes. He is not optimistic, nor even hopeful. His words come out angrily, with a vehemence that shocks some viewers. Kennedy speaks the words of a man who has been bent until he will bend no more. And now he's fighting back.

"Within the past week, unmistakable evidence has established the fact that a series of offensive missile sites is now in preparation on that imprisoned island. The purpose of these bases can be none other than to provide a nuclear strike capability against the Western Hemisphere."

Here the president pauses, letting the words sink in. He then talks about Soviet foreign minister Andrei Gromyko's visit to his office the previous Thursday, quotes Gromyko on the subject of missiles in Cuba—and then calls Gromyko a liar, for all the world to hear.

The president is about to throw down the gauntlet. "Acting, therefore, in the defense of our own security and of the entire Western Hemisphere, and under the

Top: *Soviet ship with missiles partially uncovered.* [© Bettmann/Corbis]

Bottom: *The U.S. destroyer* Vesole *escorts a Soviet ship returning to its home port, November 12, 1962.* [© Bettmann/Corbis]

authority entrusted me by the Constitution as endorsed by the resolution of the Congress, I have directed that the following initial steps be taken immediately."

JFK promises to "quarantine" Cuba, using the might of the U.S. Navy to prevent any Soviet vessel from entering Cuban waters. He declares that he is prepared to use military might in the form of an invasion, if necessary. He states unequivocally that any missile launched by the Cubans or Soviets will be considered an act of war and that the United States will reciprocate with missiles of its own.

The year before the Cuban missile crisis, Khrushchev and Kennedy had a cordial meeting in Vienna, Austria. [© Associated Press]

The president then places the blame squarely on the Soviets. "And finally, I call upon Chairman Khrushchev to halt and eliminate this clandestine, reckless, and provocative threat to world peace and stable relations between our two nations. I call upon him further to abandon this course of world domination and to join in an historic effort to end the perilous arms race and transform the history of man."

The power of the president's speech, and the terrible news that he now delivers to the public, will make this moment stand forever in the minds of people watching. For as long as they live, men and women will recall where they were and what they were doing when they heard this terrible news.

John Kennedy, being his charismatic self, is incapable of concluding a speech without a stirring moment to galvanize his listeners. Whether with his Gold Star Mothers speech in a Boston American Legion hall during his first run for Congress, or with his inaugural address in 1961, or now on national television, JFK knows how to grab his listeners by the heart and rally their emotional support.

"Our goal is not the victory of might, but the vindication of right. Not peace at the expense of freedom, but both peace and freedom—here in this hemisphere and, we hope, around the world. God willing, that goal will be achieved."

The White House set fades to black.

American forces around the world immediately prepare for war. All navy and marine personnel are about to have their duty tours extended indefinitely. American warships and submarines form a defensive perimeter around Cuba, preparing to stop and search the 25 Soviet ships currently sailing toward that defiant island.

U.S. Air Force bombers are already in the air around the clock. The crews will circle over European and American skies in a racetrack pattern, awaiting the "go" code to break from their flight plan and strike at the heart of the Soviet Union. The nonstop air brigade means just one thing: The United States is ready to retaliate and destroy Russia.

Thirteen hundred miles away from Washington, D.C., in Dallas, Texas, Lee Harvey Oswald is listening to Kennedy's speech. Unlike the majority of Americans, Oswald believes that the Soviets have every right to be in Cuba. He is convinced that President Kennedy is putting the world on the brink of nuclear war by taking such an aggressive stance against the Soviets. From Oswald's perspective, Castro's people must be protected from the terrorist behavior of the United States.

Oswald moved from Forth Worth to Dallas earlier in the month and found a job at the firm of Jaggars-Chiles-Stovall, as a photographic trainee. Amazingly, the firm has a contract with the U.S. Army Map Service that involves highly classified photographs taken by the U-2 spy planes flying over Cuba. One of Marina

Nikita Khrushchev hoped that Fidel Castro's Cuba would be a Soviet power base. [© Associated Press]

Oswald's Russian friends, George de Mohrenschildt, arranged for Oswald to be hired there. De Mohrenschildt is a mysterious character, a wealthy Russian-American businessman who just may have CIA connections. If the FBI, in all its zeal to stop the spread of communism, is concerned that a former Soviet defector now has a job with access to top-secret U-2 data at the peak of cold war tensions, the agency is not proving it by paying attention to his case.

Nor are they curious about why George de Mohrenschildt has taken an interest in the Oswalds.

—⊷⊶—

Thousands of miles away in Moscow, a furious Nikita Khrushchev composes his response to JFK's televised message.

It was Khrushchev alone who devised the plan to place missiles in Cuba. He presented his idea to the Soviet government's Central

Committee and then to Fidel Castro just three months earlier. Khrushchev claimed the decision was a goodwill gesture to the Cuban people, in case of another Bay of Pigs–style invasion. He believed the missiles could be hidden from the United States and, even if they were discovered, that Kennedy would refuse to act.

But Khrushchev is wrong about Kennedy. He is surprised to learn that his adversary is deadly serious about defending his country at all costs. Khrushchev tells associates he will not back down. He is a firm believer in the old Russian saying, "Once you're in a fight, don't spare yourself. Give it everything you've got."

On the evening of October 24, Khrushchev orders that his letter be transmitted to Kennedy. In it the Communist leader states calmly and unequivocally that the president's proposed naval blockade is "a pirate act." Soviet ships are being instructed to ignore it.

President Kennedy receives Premier Khrushchev's letter just before 11:00 P.M. on October 24. He responds less than three hours later, coolly stating that the blockade is necessary and placing all blame for the crisis on Khrushchev and the Soviets.

It's becoming clear that Kennedy will never back down.

Cuban soldiers stand by anti-aircraft artillery at the Havana, Cuba, waterfront in response to the warning of an invasion by the United States. [© Bettmann/Corbis]

CHAPTER FOURTEEN

OCTOBER 26, 1962
The White House

AS THE SOVIET LEADERSHIP WAITS FOR JFK to crack, he instead goes on the offensive. The president spends Friday, October 26, planning the invasion of Cuba. No detail is too small. He requests a list of all Cuban doctors in Miami, just in case there will be a need to airlift them into Cuba. Kennedy knows where each invasion ship will assemble. All the while, the president frets that "when military hostilities first begin, those missiles will be fired at us."

JFK is privately telling aides that it's now a showdown between him and Khrushchev, "two men sitting on opposite sides of the world," deciding "the end of civilization."

It's a staring contest. The loser is the one who blinks first.

Khrushchev spends all of that night in the Kremlin—just in case something violent transpires. The Soviet leader is uncharacteristically pensive. Something is on his mind. Shortly after

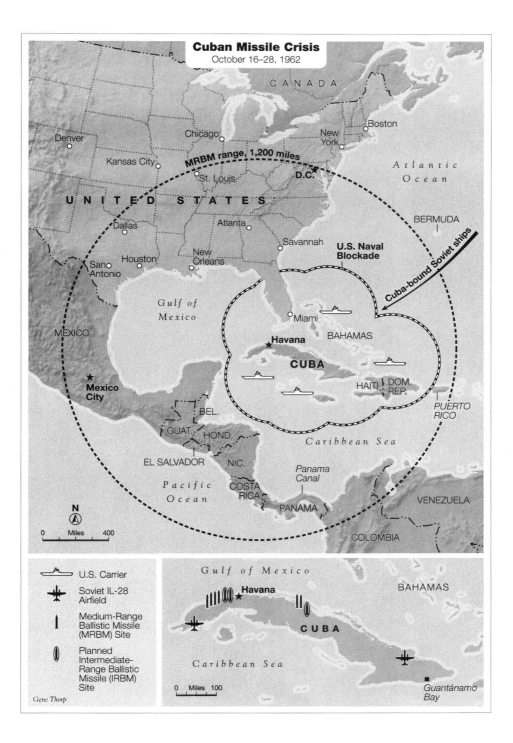

Cuban Missile Crisis
October 16–28, 1962

CANADA

Denver

Chicago

Boston

New York

Kansas City

MRBM range, 1,200 miles

St. Louis

D.C.

Atlantic Ocean

UNITED STATES

Dallas

Atlanta

Savannah

BERMUDA

San Antonio

Houston

New Orleans

U.S. Naval Blockade

Cuba-bound Soviet ships

MEXICO

Gulf of Mexico

Miami

BAHAMAS

★ Havana

Mexico City

CUBA

HAITI ⟩ DOM. REP.

PUERTO RICO

BEL.

GUAT.

HOND.

Caribbean Sea

EL SALVADOR

NIC.

Panama Canal

VENEZUELA

Pacific Ocean

COSTA RICA

PANAMA

N

COLOMBIA

0   Miles   400

Legend:

⊼ U.S. Carrier

✈ Soviet IL-28 Airfield

❙ Medium-Range Ballistic Missile (MRBM) Site

◖ Planned Intermediate-Range Ballistic Missile (IRBM) Site

Gulf of Mexico

Havana ★

BAHAMAS

CUBA

Caribbean Sea

0   Miles   100

Guantánamo Bay

Gene Thorp

midnight, he sits down and dictates a new message to President Kennedy.

It is 7:00 P.M. in Washington and 3:00 A.M. in Moscow when the message is delivered. JFK has spent the day fine-tuning the upcoming invasion of Cuba. He is bone tired, running on a hidden reserve of energy.

The same is true of the ExComm—Executive Committee of the National Security Council—men who have been working with Kennedy. They've been awake night and day for almost two weeks. Then Khrushchev's message arrives. The letter's wording is personal, an appeal from one leader to another to do the right thing. The Soviet leader insists that he is not trying to incite nuclear war: "Only lunatics or suicides, who themselves want to perish and to destroy the whole world before they die, could do this," he writes. The Soviet ruler rambles on, questioning Kennedy's motivations.

Khrushchev closes his letter by negotiating with Kennedy in a somewhat confusing fashion. The paragraph that draws the most attention states, "If, however, you have not lost your self-control and sensibly conceive what this might lead to, then, Mr. President, we and you ought not now to pull on the ends of the rope in which you have tied the knot of war, because the more the two of us pull, the tighter that knot will be tied. And a moment may come when that knot will be tied so tight that even he who tied it will not have the strength to untie it, and then it will be necessary to cut that knot. . . ."

The ExComm group does not believe that Khrushchev's

message is the sign of an outright capitulation. But they all agree it's a start.

For the first time in more than a week, Kennedy feels hopeful. Yet he does not lift the blockade. There are still nearly a dozen Soviet vessels steering directly toward the quarantine line—and these ships show no signs of turning around.

The tension increases the next afternoon, when word reaches the president that Cuban surface-to-air missiles have shot down an American U-2 spy plane. The pilot, Major Rudolf Anderson Jr., has been killed.

In retaliation, the Joint Chiefs of Staff demand that the president launch U.S. bombers in a massive air strike on Cuba within 48 hours, to be followed by an outright invasion.

President Kennedy secretly sends Bobby to meet with Soviet officials in Washington with the promise not to invade Cuba if the missiles are removed.

Then Khrushchev blinks.

The Communist leader has been so sure that Kennedy is bluffing that he has not mobilized the Soviet army to full alert. Yet Khrushchev's intelligence reports now show that the United States is serious about invading Cuba.

The Russian dictator sees that the American president is willing to conduct a nuclear war if pushed to the limit. Yes, the United States will be gone forever. But so will the Soviet Union.

On Sunday morning, at nine o'clock, Radio Moscow tells the people of the Soviet Union that Chairman Khrushchev has saved the world from annihilation. The words are also aimed directly at JFK when the commentator states that the Soviets choose to "dismantle the arms which you described as offensive, and to crate and return them to Soviet Russia."

After 13 exhausting days, the Cuban missile crisis is over.

In Dallas, Lee Harvey Oswald has been following the action closely. He is living alone in the new two-story brick apartment he rented on Elsbeth Street. After the couple had many fights, Marina moved in with some of her Russian friends and hasn't even given Oswald her new address.

Outcast, misunderstood, and alone, Lee Harvey Oswald, who considers himself a great man destined to accomplish great things, festers in a quiet rage.

Oswald very rarely smiled for photographs. [© Corbis]

CHAPTER FIFTEEN

JANUARY 8, 1963
Washington, D.C. 9:30 P.M.

JACKIE KENNEDY LOOKS STUNNING in her pink gown and dangling diamond earrings. Long white gloves come up past her elbows. She makes small talk with a man she adores, André Malraux, the 61-year-old writer who serves as the French minister of culture.

On this night, as she stands in the West Sculpture Hall of the National Gallery of Art, the first lady is truly a vision.

Jackie turns away from Malraux to gaze at the figure in the painting hanging on the gallery wall. She is known as *La Gioconda*, or the *Mona Lisa*, a wife and mother of five children who sat for this portrait by Leonardo da Vinci in the early sixteenth century.

Bringing the world's most famous painting to Washington, D.C., has been Jackie's dream. About a year ago, she made a discreet request to Malraux, who then arranged the loan.

Now millions of Americans will line up to view the painting before its return to France in March—and all because of Jackie Kennedy.

John Walker, director of the National Gallery, was against the loan, fearful that his career would be ruined if he failed to protect the *Mona Lisa* from theft or the damage that might accompany moving a fragile, 460-year-old painting across an ocean in the dead of winter.

Walker's task of protecting the painting at the gallery was made much easier when JFK ordered the world's most elite bodyguards to watch over the precious work of art—none other than the men who would willingly take a bullet to protect the president himself: the Secret Service.

The Mona Lisa *has just arrived from France. It will remain in a vault deep below the National Gallery until it goes on view.*
[© Bettmann/Corbis]

John and Jackie stand before the Mona Lisa. *With them are French Minister of Culture André Malraux; his wife, Marie-Madeleine; and Vice President Johnson.* [JFK Presidential Library and Museum]

Of course the Secret Service's primary responsibility is to ensure the safety of the president, vice president, and other important government officials and dignitaries. Secret Service officers have a special language, including code names for people and places. The president's Secret Service code name is Lancer. The first lady's is Lace. Caroline and John are Lyric and Lark, respectively. Almost

Jackie beams with pleasure at the opening of the exhibit, with Hervé Alphand, the French ambassador to the U.S., and his wife, Nicole.
[JFK Presidential Library and Museum]

everything and everyone in the first family's lives has a code name: LBJ is Volunteer; the presidential car, a Lincoln, is SS-100-X; and the White House itself is Castle. Most subsets of names and places begin with the same first letter: *L* for the first family, *W* for the White House staff, and *D* for Secret Service agents.

John Kennedy's bodyguards carry .38 revolvers that bulge beneath their suit coats. The Secret Service's motto is "Worthy of trust and confidence," and the agents reinforce that message through their poise and professionalism. They are athletic men, many of them with college degrees and military backgrounds. There are eight agents on each of the three eight-hour shifts, and every agent is trained to handle a variety of deadly weapons. The Secret Service headquarters in the White House is a small windowless office at the north entrance to the West Wing, where an armory of riot guns and Thompson submachine guns provides additional firepower. There are several layers of security between JFK and a potential assassin, beginning at the White House gates and

A Secret Service agent is only steps behind even when the first lady is shopping. [© Bettmann/Corbis]

Sometimes Secret Service agents spend time on the playground.
Robert Foster plays with John Jr. [JFK Presidential Library and Museum]

continuing right up to the black-and-white-tiled hallway outside the Oval Office, where an agent remains on duty whenever the president is working. Should Kennedy need to summon that agent at a moment's notice, the president can push a special emergency button beneath his desk.

The easiest place to attack the president is outside the White House. Anytime he leaves, eight Secret Service agents travel ahead of the president to survey his upcoming location. They form a human shield around him as he moves.

For those protecting the president, JFK's almost manic activity is the toughest part of the job. He likes to appear vigorous in public and often risks his life by wading deep into crowds to shake hands. These moments terrify his security detail. Any crazed lunatic with a gun and an agenda could easily take a shot during times like those. Should that happen, each agent is prepared to place his body between the bullet and the president, sacrificing his own life for the good of the country.

It helps that the agents truly like JFK. He knows them by name

Kennedy throws out the first ball of the 1962 baseball season on opening day at D.C. Stadium. [JFK Presidential Library and Museum]

The first lady arrives for a luncheon in her honor. The head of her Secret Service detail, Clint Hill, is on the far right.
[JFK Presidential Library and Museum]

and is fond of bantering with them. Despite this familiarity, the men of the Secret Service never forget that John Kennedy is the president of the United States. Their sense of decorum is evident in the respectful way they address Kennedy. Face-to-face, they call him Mr. President. When two agents talk about him, he is known as "the boss." And when speaking to visitors or guests, they refer to him as President Kennedy.

These Secret Service agents are also very fond of Jackie. The agent in charge of her detail, six-foot-tall Clint Hill (code name Dazzle), has become her close friend and confidant.

Thus, it is almost natural that Secret Service protection be extended to the *Mona Lisa*. The passionate crowds who will surround da Vinci's painting are similar to the throngs who scream for JFK and Jackie on their travels around the world.

That is why the Secret Service never lets down its guard.

Not yet, at least.

—⬤—

If the Secret Service is aware of Lee Harvey Oswald, that fact is nowhere in any record.

Their ignorance is not unusual. Why would the powerful Secret Service be watching a low-level former marine living in Dallas, Texas?

Oswald's life continues to be defined by a balance of passion and rage. Marina has moved back in with him. On January 27, 1963, as crowds 10 abreast line the streets of Washington to view the *Mona Lisa*, Oswald orders a .38 Special revolver through the mail. It costs him $29.95. Oswald slides a $10 bill into the envelope, with the balance to be paid on delivery. He keeps the purchase a secret from Marina by having the gun sent to a post office box.

Oswald has no special plans for his new pistol. Nobody has been making threats on his life, and for now he has no intention of killing anyone. He merely likes the idea of owning a gun—just in case.

Lee Harvey Oswald is growing more isolated. He has turned a closet in his home into an office. There he writes angrily about the world around him. He becomes increasingly agitated, and people are beginning to fear him.

On March 12 in Dallas, Oswald decides to buy a second gun. This time it's a rifle. He buys an Italian Mannlicher-Carcano gun that was made in 1940 and originally designed for Italian infantry use during World War II. This is not a gun designed for hunting animals, but for shooting men. As a former Marine Corps sharpshooter, Oswald knows how to clean, maintain, load, aim, and accurately fire such a weapon.

The rifle arrives on March 25. Marina complains that they could have used the money for food. But Oswald is pleased with the purchase and gets in the habit of riding the bus to a dry riverbed for target practice.

On March 31, while Marina is hanging diapers on the clothesline to dry, Oswald steps into the backyard dressed all in black. His new pistol is tucked into his belt. He waves the rifle in one hand and holds copies of two Communist newspapers in the other. He demands that an amused Marina take photographs of him. He plans to send them to the newspapers to show that he is prepared to do anything to support communism.

On April 6, 1963, Lee Harvey Oswald is fired from his job at Jaggars-Chiles-Stovall. His communist rants have grown offensive to coworkers, and his bosses claim he has become undependable.

On April 10, 1963, Oswald decides it's time to kill someone.

Lee Harvey Oswald in his yard, holding his rifle and newspapers. [© Corbis]

CHAPTER SIXTEEN

APRIL 1963

Washington, D.C.

THE MAN WITH SEVEN MONTHS TO LIVE is thinking about a faraway war that is gaining steam.

Dwight Eisenhower was the first president to send American soldiers to Vietnam. He and his advisers were afraid that if Vietnam became communist, the countries around it would, too, and then all of Southeast Asia would turn its back on democracy. But it is John Kennedy who orders a gradual escalation in the number of troops, hoping to ensure that Vietnam does not fall.

Kennedy's good intentions have gone awry, however. The original handful of American "advisers" in Vietnam has now swelled to almost 16,000 pilots and soldiers. They hope to destroy the rebel Viet Cong army that is fighting the U.S.-backed Vietnam government. Thousands of Viet Cong soldiers have been killed—as have thousands of innocent Vietnamese citizens.

John Kennedy believes that America needs to end the

Soon after taking office, Kennedy gave the press an update on Communist-held areas in Southeast Asia. [JFK Presidential Library and Museum]

Vietnam conflict, though he is not quite ready to go public with this. "We don't have a prayer of staying in Vietnam," he will tell Pulitzer Prize–winning journalist Charles Bartlett off the record. "Those people hate us. They are going to throw [us] out of there at almost any point. But I can't give up a piece of territory like that to the Communists and then get the American people to reelect me."

To safeguard his chances for staying in office, the president cannot, and will not, pull U.S. troops out of Vietnam until after the 1964 election. The war is still popular with voters.

CHAPTER SEVENTEEN

APRIL 10, 1963
Dallas, Texas

O N A HOT APRIL NIGHT, Lee Harvey Oswald hides in the shadows of a Dallas alleyway. His new rifle is pointed at Major General Ted Walker. The 53-year-old West Point graduate is a famous opponent of communism. One of the communist newspapers Oswald subscribes to has targeted the general as dangerous to its beliefs because he publicly warns Americans about the threat of communism.

Lee Harvey Oswald finds strength in the ideals of communism. He believes that the profit from everybody's work should be shared equally by all. He thinks if the country were organized that way, then there would be no poor people and everyone would be equal. Perhaps he has forgotten his experiences in the factory in Russia where he was so unhappy.

After almost a year back home in America, he has become enraged by what he perceives as the injustices he sees around him. He is angry enough to kill any man who speaks out against communism.

This is why he is aiming his brand-new rifle with murderous intent at Ted Walker's head.

Walker sits in the study of his Dallas home looking at his 1962 tax returns. The desk lamp is the room's only light. A small window looks out into the darkness.

Lee Harvey Oswald's hiding spot in the alley is just 40 yards away. He watches Walker's every move through the telescopic sight of his rifle. The sight is so strong that Oswald can see every strand of hair on Walker's head. He takes

Former Major General Edwin A. "Ted" Walker speaks with reporters the morning after a bullet narrowly missed him. [© Bettmann/Corbis]

aim. He has never shot a man before, or even fired a gun in anger. But he spent hours on the firing range back in his Marine Corps days, and these last few weeks he has been diligently working on his accuracy down in the dry bed of the Trinity River.

Oswald squeezes the trigger. He fires just one shot. Then he turns and runs as fast and as far as he can.

A photo of General Walker's house that was in Lee Harvey Oswald's wallet when he was arrested. [© Corbis]

"I shot Walker," Oswald breathlessly tells Marina. It's 11:30 at night. She has been worried sick about his absence.

"Did you kill him?" she asks.

"I don't know," he replies in Russian.

"What did you do with the rifle?"

"Buried it."

Oswald turns on the radio to see if he's made the news yet.

The Walker assassination attempt is in the newspapers and on the radio the next morning. Oswald hangs on every word, though he is appalled to learn that he missed his target completely. Eyewitnesses claim they saw two men fleeing the scene in a car, and Dallas police are looking for a gun that takes a completely different sort of ammunition from the kind Oswald fired. Oswald is crestfallen. He shot at Walker because he wanted to be a hero in the eyes of the Communist Party; he wanted to be special. Now not only has he botched the shot, but he is worse than a failure—he is anonymous.

On April 21, Marina sees Oswald getting ready to leave the house with a pistol tucked in his waistband. It's a Sunday. He's wearing a suit. Marina furiously demands to know where he's going. "Nixon is coming," Oswald tells her. "I'm going to go check it out."

The former vice president has just made headlines in the morning paper by demanding the removal of all Communists from Cuba. Like General Walker, Richard Nixon has been making a political name for himself by denouncing Communists.

"I know how you look," Marina says. Her husband's idea of checking out a situation is to fire a shot at a human being. Marina Oswald shoves her husband into their tiny bathroom and forces him to remain there for the rest of the day. By the time she sets him free, Marina hopes that Nixon has left Dallas.

CHAPTER EIGHTEEN

THE WHITE HOUSE
Washington, D.C.

DESPITE THE CRISES AND LONG HOURS, John Kennedy truly enjoys his job, and it shows. Friends note how much he has grown as a leader during his time in office and the energy with which he tackles his work.

But there is a flip side to the president's popularity polls: 70 percent of the nation may love JFK, but the other 30 percent hate him. In Miami, many in the Cuban exile community are bitter about the Bay of Pigs debacle and want revenge. In the South, rage at the president's push for racial equality is widespread.

JFK is aware of his enemies but

The public lives of the president and his wife required many dinners, parties, and ceremonial occasions. [JFK Presidential Library and Museum]

Private time and vacations were few and much cherished by the family. Kennedy loved being on the water. Here he is aboard a U.S. Coast Guard boat off the coast of Maine. [JFK Presidential Library and Museum]

The family at their Cape Cod vacation home, August 4, 1962. [JFK Presidential Library and Museum]

is also conscious of the positive news people read each day in the headlines: Gordon Cooper completes America's longest space flight, orbiting Earth 22 times; the U.S. crop harvest exceeds expectations; Peace Corps volunteers reach 7,000; and the world hails Kennedy's prodemocracy speech at the Berlin Wall.

Despite all the good news, as the year goes on, John Kennedy will be forced to use every bit of his presidential skill to manage a situation that is getting to the boiling point: the civil rights struggle.

Kennedy was the first president to conduct televised live press conferences that were not edited or delayed. By November 1963 he would hold sixty-four press conferences.
[JFK Presidential Library and Museum]

CHAPTER NINETEEN

MAY 3, 1963
Birmingham, Alabama 1:00 P.M.

"**W**E'RE GOING TO WALK, WALK, WALK. Freedom . . . Freedom . . . Freedom," the protesters chant as they march out through the great oak doors of the Sixteenth Street Baptist Church. It is a Friday, and these young black students should be in school. Instead, they have gathered to march for civil rights. Some are less than 10 years old. Most are teenagers. They are football players, homecoming queens, track stars, and cheerleaders.

The marchers number more than 1,000 strong. All have skipped class to be here. Their goal is to experience something their parents have never known for a single day of their lives: an integrated Birmingham, where lunch counters, department stores, public restrooms, and water fountains are open to all. The protesters plan to march into the white business district and peacefully enter stores and restaurants.

The Children's Crusade, as *Newsweek* magazine will call it,

Restrooms, drinking fountains, buses, and movie theaters were segregated in many places in the South in the 1960s. [© Bob Adelman/Corbis]

fans out across acre-wide Kelly Ingram Park. "We're going to walk, walk, walk," they continue to chant.

They know that this march is not just about public toilets; this march is an act of defiance. Just four months ago, George Wallace became governor of Alabama. At his inaugural, he proclaimed, "In the name of the greatest people that have ever trod this earth, I draw the line in the dust and toss the gauntlet before the feet of tyranny. And I say segregation now, segregation tomorrow, segregation forever!" Those words were a call to arms for blacks and whites alike who disagreed with Wallace.

The Children's Crusade has now reached the shade of Kelly Ingram Park's elm trees. The temperature is a humid 80 degrees. Ahead, the marchers see barricades and rows of fire trucks. German shepherds, trained by the police to attack, bark and snarl at the approach of the young students, and an enormous crowd of black and white spectators lines the east side of the park, waiting to see what will happen next.

Martin Luther King Jr. speaks to the protesters before they set out from the church, reminding them that jail is a small price to pay for a good cause. They know not to fight back against the police or otherwise provoke confrontation when challenged. Their efforts will be in vain if the march turns into a riot.

Eugene "Bull" Connor is Birmingham's public safety commissioner. A former Ku Klux Klan member, he is a strict segregationist. He can't afford to let these kids get to the white shopping district. He has ordered Birmingham firefighters to attach their hoses to hydrants and be ready to open those nozzles and spray water on the marchers at full force—a power so great that it can remove the bark from trees or mortar from a brick building. If the protesters reach the shopping district, using the hoses might damage expensive storefronts. The marchers need to be stopped now.

The first children in the group are met with a half-strength blast from the fire hoses. It's still enough force to stop many of them in their tracks. Some of the kids simply sit down and let the water batter them, following orders not to be violent or to retreat.

Connor, realizing that half measures will not work with these determined children, then gives the order to spray at full strength. All the protesters are knocked off their feet. Many children are swept away down the streets and sidewalks, their bodies scraping against grass and concrete. Clothing is torn from their bodies. Those who make the mistake of pressing themselves against a building to dodge the hoses soon become perfect targets. "The water stung like a whip and hit like a cannon," one protester will later remember. "The force of it knocked you down like you weighed only

Firefighters turn their hoses full force on civil rights demonstrators on July 15, 1963, in Birmingham, Alabama. [Bill Hudson/AP]

twenty pounds, pushing people around like rag dolls. We tried to hold on to the building, but that was no use."

Then Connor lets loose the police dogs.

Bull Connor watches as the German shepherds lunge at the children, ripping away their clothing and tearing into their flesh.

By 3:00 P.M., it all seems to be over. The children who haven't been arrested limp home in their soaked and torn clothing, their bodies bruised by point-blank blasts from the water cannons. No longer bold and defiant, they are now just a bunch of kids who have to explain to their angry parents about their ruined clothes and a missed day of school.

Bull Connor has won. Or at least it seems that way.

But among those in Birmingham this afternoon is an Associated Press photographer named Bill Hudson. He is considered one of the best in the business, willing to endure any danger to get a great photo. On this day, Bill Hudson takes the best photo of his life. It is an image of a Birmingham police officer—looking official in pressed shirt, tie, and sunglasses—holding a leash while his German shepherd lunges toward black high school student Walter Gadsden.

Walter Gadsden, a seventeen-year-old demonstrator, is attacked by a police dog. This photograph enraged people across the country. [Bill Hudson/AP]

Next page: *Young marchers head toward Kelly Ingram Park. They will become important symbols of the civil rights movement.* [© Bob Adelman/Magnum Photos]

The next morning, that photograph appears on the front page of the *New York Times*, three columns wide.

And so it is that John Kennedy, starting his morning as he always does by reading the papers, sees this image from Birmingham. Just one look, and JFK instinctively knows that America and the world will be outraged by Hudson's image. Civil rights are sure to be a major issue of the 1964 presidential election. And Kennedy now understands he can no longer be a passive observer of the civil rights movement. He must take a stand—no matter how many votes it might lose him in the South.

Kennedy makes a point of telling reporters that the picture is "sick" and "shameful."

Petitions from around the country, including this one from California, arrived at the White House urging President Kennedy to support the goals of Martin Luther King Jr.'s nonviolent protests in Birmingham. The petition asks the president "to call for nationwide prayers and national unity of purpose to secure and protect the rights of every citizen under our Constitution. . . ."
[JFK Presidential Library and Museum]

CHAPTER TWENTY

JUNE 22, 1963
Washington, D.C. Late Morning

THE PRESIDENT AND **M**ARTIN **L**UTHER **K**ING **J**R. walk alone through the White House Rose Garden. This is the first time they've met. Kennedy towers over the five-foot-six civil rights leader. Today is a Saturday and the start of a carefully orchestrated series of meetings between the White House and some powerful business groups to mobilize support for the civil rights movement.

John Kennedy has thrown the power of his office behind the civil rights movement, but reluctantly. It is Bobby Kennedy who is the driving force behind his brother's new stand.

May 1963 was a trying month, marked by confrontation after confrontation in Birmingham, spurred by Governor George Wallace. In June, after successfully ensuring that the University of Alabama was integrated, JFK delivered a nationally televised address about civil rights. In a hastily written and partially improvised speech that would one day be counted among his best, the president promised that his administration would do everything it could to end segregation. He pushed Congress to "enact legislation giving all Americans the right to be served in facilities open to the public."

Integration, however, is not just a matter of doing the right thing. JFK's commitment has far-reaching ramifications. For instance, some Americans think that it is Communists who are supporting the civil rights movement. The last thing Kennedy wants is to be branded a Communist, even though he knows that many in the South think he is.

And there is another painful truth: Unlike the Cuban missile crisis or even the failed Bay of Pigs invasion, the civil rights situation is a problem over which John Kennedy has little direct control. Martin Luther King Jr. is on the front line in this battle. It is King who is in command—and both men know it.

These two politically savvy leaders share a goal. The president warns King to be careful: "If they shoot you down, they'll shoot us down, too."

Martin Luther King Jr. has five more years to live.

John Fitzgerald Kennedy has precisely five months.

On June 22, 1963, civil rights leaders meet with Vice President Johnson and Attorney General Robert Kennedy at the White House. Martin Luther King Jr. is to the left of Kennedy. [JFK Presidential Library and Museum]

CHAPTER TWENTY-ONE

SUMMER 1963

New Orleans, Louisiana

L EE HARVEY OSWALD HAS A PASSION in the summer of
1963: reading.

After he shot at Walker and developed an interest in Nixon,
Marina decided that they should leave Dallas for New Orleans.
Oswald spends the month of June working as a maintenance
man for the Reily Coffee Company there. His employers are
not thrilled with his job performance, complaining that he
spends too many of his working hours reading gun magazines.

Marina knows that her husband is applying for a visa that
could return them to the Soviet Union, even though she doesn't
want to go. In fact, because he is applying separately for his own
visa, it appears he may be trying to send Marina, who is again
pregnant, and their daughter, June, back to Russia without him.

Lee Harvey Oswald is far from the great man he believes he
will one day become. Right now he is a drifter who spends his

time off trying to make wine from blackberries, barely clinging to employment, and treating his family like a nuisance.

Reading fuels Oswald's rage. He devours several books a week. The topics range in subject matter from a Chairman Mao biography to James Bond novels. Then, during the first weeks of summer 1963, Oswald chooses to read about a subject he's never before explored: John F. Kennedy.

In fact, Lee Harvey is so enchanted by William Manchester's bestseller *Portrait of a President* that after returning it to the New Orleans Public Library, he checks out Kennedy's *Profiles in Courage*.

The collection of essays,

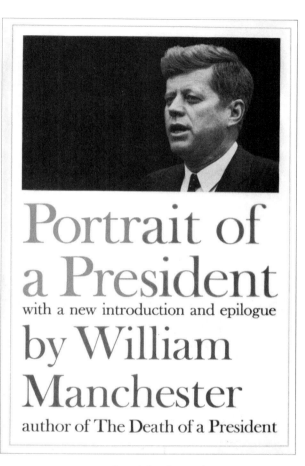

Portrait of a President

with a new introduction and epilogue

by William Manchester

author of The Death of a President

Kennedy said that this was his favorite book about himself. After the assassination, Manchester wrote an in-depth description of Kennedy's last days.
[Courtesy of Little, Brown and Company]

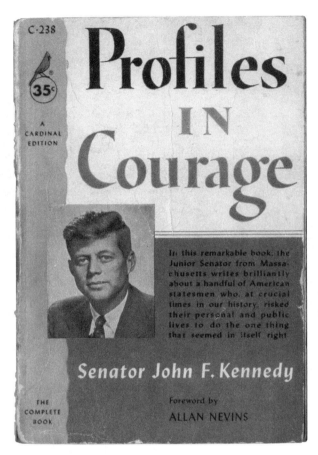

which won John Kennedy the Pulitzer Prize in 1957, is about the lives and actions of eight great men. Lee Harvey Oswald reads JFK's carefully chosen words and is inspired to hope that one day he, too, will exhibit that sort of courage.

Profiles in Courage *was published in 1957 when Kennedy was a senator. Kennedy writes about eight senators who acted bravely and honestly in hard situations.*
[© Cardinal Publishers Group]

CHAPTER TWENTY-TWO

AUGUST 28, 1963
Washington, D.C. Afternoon

"FIVE SCORE YEARS AGO, A GREAT AMERICAN, in whose symbolic shadow we stand today, signed the Emancipation Proclamation," begins Martin Luther King Jr.

The huge statue of Abraham Lincoln in the Lincoln Memorial is right behind King. It has been one hundred years since Lincoln freed the slaves, and now King is telling a crowd of hundreds of thousands that black Americans are still not free.

He talks about poverty and the fact that America separates black from white.

Many in the crowd have traveled hundreds of miles to be here today. They are black, and they are white. The day has been long, filled with hours of speeches.

But Martin Luther King Jr. is the man they've waited to hear. And the fatigue and the heat and the claustrophobia are all forgotten as these 250,000 people strain to hear his every word. They have come for the cause of civil rights, but they have also come to hear the great orator shape this day for them. The audience know in their hearts that King will rally them to greatness.

"We cannot be satisfied as long as a Negro in Mississippi cannot vote and a Negro in New York believes he has nothing for which to vote," Martin Luther King Jr. preaches.

And then, for the first time, he belts out the phrase that will come to define this day forever.

"I have a dream!" King proclaims.

And then he tells them about that dream. King describes an earthly paradise where blacks and whites are not divided. He dreams that even a hostile Southern state like Mississippi will know such wonders.

He is putting into words the ultimate goal of the civil rights movement. And for the people in the crowd to hear it stated so powerfully and clearly has them beside themselves with emotion and pride. Black and white alike, they hang on every word of King's 16-minute speech.

By the time King winds up for the finish, he is shouting into the microphone. The image of Lincoln gazing over his shoulder is profoundly moving as King calls upon the spirit of the Emancipation Proclamation. It is clear to all who stand out on the Mall that King plans to finish what Lincoln began so long ago. The two men—divided by a century of racial injustice—are forever linked in history from this day forward.

Martin Luther King Jr. acknowledges the crowd of marchers on August 28, 1963. [© Associated Press]

"Free at last, free at last," he quotes from a spiritual, "thank God almighty, we are free at last."

The crowd on the Mall erupts in applause.

President Kennedy meets with the organizers of the March on Washington in the Oval Office after Martin Luther King Jr. (third from the left) gave his speech. [© Associated Press]

In the White House, John Kennedy watches King's speech on television with Bobby and their brother Teddy, who was elected to John's former Senate seat for Massachusetts in 1962.

The attorney general is a major advocate for the civil rights movement. Since King announced the March on Washington three months ago, Bobby has become its behind-the-scenes organizer. Working closely with his staff at the Justice Department, Bobby has quietly guided the march into a shape that can be easily controlled. He made sure that the Lincoln Memorial was the site of King's speech, because it is bordered on one side by the Potomac River and on the other by the Tidal Basin. This would make crowd control smoother in case of riots and also keep marchers away from the Capitol Building and the White House.

The president and his brothers watch King's speech with interest, praying that he will deliver on the promise of this great march on Washington.

One hour later, an exultant Martin Luther King Jr. meets with John Kennedy in the Oval Office. There are 11 other people in attendance, so this visit is not a summit meeting between the president of the United States and the most powerful man in the civil rights movement. But Kennedy makes sure King knows he's been paying attention to the day's events.

"I have a dream," he says to King, adding a nod of the head to show approval.

CHAPTER TWENTY-THREE

SEPTEMBER 15, 1963

Birmingham, Alabama

B UT THE MARCH ON WASHINGTON does not change the ongoing racial battle in the American South. Less than three weeks after America listened to Martin Luther King Jr. dream about black boys and girls in Alabama joining hands with white boys and girls, 26 black children are led into the basement of the Sixteenth Street Baptist Church for Sunday morning services. They are due to hear a children's sermon on "The Love That Forgives."

The Sixteenth Street Baptist Church is the same congregation that launched the Children's Crusade on Birmingham in May 1963. It stands just across from the park where Bull Connor's police dogs bit into the flesh of innocent black teenagers and elementary school students. The church has earned a special level of hatred from the white supremacist groups that still battle to block the integration of Birmingham.

The children attending church this Sunday morning cannot

The victims of the Sixteenth Street Baptist Church bombing (clockwise from top left):
Denise McNair, 11; Carole Robertson, 14; Cynthia Wesley, 14; and
Addie Mae Collins, 14. [© Associated Press]

This stained-glass window was partially intact after the bombing that killed four children and injured twenty-three others. [LOC, DIG-highsm-05062]

possibly know that four members of the Ku Klux Klan have planted a box of dynamite near the basement. The force of the explosion that shatters the spiritual calm of the church service at 10:22 A.M. is so great that it doesn't just destroy the basement, but also blows out the back wall of the church and destroys every stained-glass window in the building but one. That lone surviving window portrays an image of Jesus; all but the face of the figure remains intact.

The window is symbolic in a sense, because most of the children in the basement this Sunday morning survive the horrific tragedy. However, four of them—Addie Mae Collins, Cynthia Wesley, Carole Robertson, and Denise McNair—do not.

Their dream has come to an end.

CHAPTER TWENTY-FOUR

SEPTEMBER 25, 1963
Billings, Montana Late afternoon

EVEN IN THE MIDST OF TRAGEDY, Kennedy must campaign. He stands in the rodeo ring at the Yellowstone County Fairgrounds, addressing an overflowing crowd. Billings, Montana, has a population of just 53,000, and it appears as if every single citizen has come out to cheer the president. A marching band adds to the pageantry.

It seems that JFK might just win Montana if the election were held tomorrow. And success in the West is a vital part of Kennedy's reelection strategy. A win in Texas, for example, would almost guarantee his victory in 1964.

And so Appointments Secretary Kenny O'Donnell has selected November 21 and 22 as the likely dates of Kennedy's eagerly anticipated Texas fund-raising trip.

The president envisions a grand tour of the state, with stops in five major cities: San Antonio, Fort Worth, Dallas, Houston, and Austin. Texas governor John Connally, a conservative

JFK surrounded by Secret Service personnel deep in a crowd in Billings, Montana, in September 1963. [JFK Presidential Library and Museum]

Democrat who has been maintaining a discreet political distance from the president, is quietly in favor of a less ambitious itinerary. Dallas, for instance, is not Kennedy territory.

The president will discuss this issue, along with other details of the trip, with John Connally next week at the White House. One statistic about the Texas trip is most glaring of all: More than 62 percent of Dallas voters did not vote for John Kennedy in 1960.

But JFK loves a challenge. If Billings, Montana, can be won over, then why not Dallas—the "Big D"?

Kenny O'Donnell (right) often accompanied the president on official trips. Here he and Pierre Salinger, Kennedy's press secretary, visit a military base in North Carolina. [JFK Presidential Library and Museum]

CHAPTER TWENTY-FIVE

SEPTEMBER–OCTOBER 1963
Texas and Mexico City

WHILE **PRESIDENT KENNEDY IS SPEAKING** in Montana, Lee Harvey Oswald is already on his way to Texas—and beyond. He is on a bus bound for Houston. From there, he will change buses and go south to Mexico City.

Oswald is traveling like a man who is never coming back. He has no home, because he has just abandoned his squalid New Orleans apartment. When the landlady came around demanding the $17 he owed in back rent, Oswald put her off with a lie and later sneaked out in the dead of night.

The sum of Oswald's worldly possessions is now divided among his wallet and the two cloth suitcases stowed in the bus's luggage bay.

As for a family, Oswald no longer has one. Two days ago he sent the very pregnant Marina and 19-month-old June to live with Marina's Quaker friend Ruth Paine, outside Dallas.

CONSULADO DE CUBA, MEXICO, D.F.

Solicitud de visa No.: 779

Fecha: 27 de septiembre de 1963.

Nombre: Lee Harvey Oswald

Ciudadanía: norteamericana

Fecha y lugar de nacimiento: Octubre 18, 1939 en New Orleans, E.U.A.

Pasaporte No. D-092526

Dirección permanente: 4907 Magazine St. Dallas, Tex., E.U.A.

Ocupación (expresando empresa para la que trabaja) Fotografo Comercial

Estancias anteriores en Cuba ---

Motivos de las estancias anteriores ---

Familiares o personas conocidas residentes en Cuba

10 OCT. 1963

¿Ha sido invitado desde Cuba? (Sí:) (No:)

Con qué objeto? ----

Cual es el motivo del viaje propuesto viaje de transito para la Unión Sovietica

... mismo 2 semanas si es posible más tiempo.

Fecha propuesta de llegada a Cuba septiembre 30 de 1963

Dirección en Cuba:

Lee H. Oswald
(firma del interesado)

PARA USO DE LA MISION

OBSERVACIONES El solicitante dice ser miembro del P.C. Norteamericano y Secretario en New Orleans del Fair Play for Cuba Committee. Y que vivió en la Unión Sovietica desde Octubre de 1959 al 19 de junio de 1962; que allá se casó con una ciudadana sovietica. Mostró documentación que lo acredita como miembro de las dos organizaciones mencionadas y acta de matrimonio. Se presentó en la Embajada de la URSS en esta ciudad pidiendo que su visa sea enviada a dicha Embajada en Cuba. Nosotros llamamos al Consulado de la URSS y nos contestaron que ellos tenían que esperar la autorización de Moscú para dar la visa y que tardaría alrededor de

The application Lee Harvey Oswald filled out in Mexico asking for a visa to go to Cuba. [Charles Tasnadi/AP]

Oswald distributing flyers in New Orleans. [© Corbis]

George de Mohrenschildt had once again intervened to help the Oswalds. He introduced them to Ruth Paine.

Ruth Paine speaks a smattering of Russian, which helps to make Marina feel more at home. Marina has stored all the family possessions in Paine's garage. Among them is a green-and-brown rolled blanket in which Lee Harvey Oswald's rifle is concealed. Ruth Paine, being a peace-loving Quaker, would never allow the gun in her garage, but she has no idea it's there.

Oswald has hatched a clever new scheme—one that doesn't involve Marina. He dreams of living in the palm-tree-fringed workers' paradise of Cuba. But it's impossible to get a Cuban travel visa in the United States because the United States and Cuba have severed diplomatic relations. So Oswald is taking the bus to Mexico City in order to apply at the Cuban embassy there.

Lee Harvey Oswald never fits in, no matter where he goes. He is constantly searching for a place where he can belong, a place that will allow him to be the great man he so longs to be. Oswald believes that Cuba is such a place. And in his mind he has done plenty to impress the Cuban dictator, Fidel Castro. Oswald spent time in New Orleans passing out leaflets for the Fair Play for Cuba Committee, a group that wants the United States to end its economic boycott of Cuba. He feels that should prove his loyalty to communism.

At 2:00 A.M. on the morning of September 27, Lee Harvey Oswald changes buses in Houston. When

HANDS OFF CUBA!

Join the Fair Play for Cuba Committee

NEW ORLEANS CHARTER MEMBER BRANCH

Free Literature, Lectures

LOCATION:

L. H. OSWALD
4907 MAGAZINE ST
NEW ORLEANS, LA.

EVERYONE WELCOME!

The Committee flyer.
[NARA/JFK Assassination Records]

he arrives in Mexico City at 10:00 A.M., Oswald checks in at the Hotel del Comercio, just four blocks from the bus station, at a rate of $1.28 per night. And though exhausted after the grueling 20-hour bus ride, he walks immediately to the Cuban embassy.

Four months. Four long months. That's how long it will take for Lee Harvey Oswald to obtain a Soviet visa, which it turns out he needs before Cuban officials will grant him travel documents.

Oswald doesn't have enough money to wait four months. He needs to go to Cuba now.

And so he stands toe-to-toe with consul Eusebio Azcue at the Cuban consulate in Mexico City, arguing with him over the Soviet visa. Finally, Azcue has had enough, and he speaks candidly with the American. "A person like you," Azcue tells Oswald in fractured English, "in the place of aiding the Cuban Revolution, are doing it harm."

Azcue concludes by telling Oswald that he will never get the paperwork to enter Cuba.

The consul turns back to his office, leaving Oswald crushed. His dream of escaping to Cuba is over. A despondent Oswald spends the weekend in Mexico City, eating local food and taking in a bullfight. But his despair is growing.

He then takes the bus back to Dallas, where he rents a room at

The Texas School Book Depository in Dallas, Texas.
All Texas public schools use the same textbooks.
They were stored and mailed out from here. [LOC, HS 503-3349]

the YMCA and looks for work. He sheepishly phones Marina at Ruth Paine's home. She is due to deliver their second baby any day.

Oswald entertains Marina with tales of Mexico, but also admits that his trip was a failure. Marina listens and believes that there is a change for the better in her husband. But she refuses to live with him. So, while looking for work, he phones his wife when he can and sometimes hitchhikes from Dallas out to the Paine residence to see her.

Finally, thanks to a kindly reference from Ruth Paine, he finds a job. It is menial labor for a man with Oswald's relatively high IQ of 118 and involves nothing more than placing books into boxes for shipping. At 8:00 A.M. on Wednesday, October 16, Lee Harvey Oswald reports for his first day on the job at the Texas School Book Depository. The seven-floor red-brick Dallas warehouse is located on the corner of Elm and North Houston and overlooks Dealey Plaza.

PART THREE

DALLAS, TEXAS
NOVEMBER 1963

CHAPTER TWENTY-SIX

NOVEMBER 1963
Dallas, Texas

KNOWN AS THE **"BIG D,"** Dallas is a dusty, dry town, miserably hot in the summer and cool in the winter. It is surrounded by some of the most unremarkable scenery in America. It is a hard city, built on business and oil, and driven by just one thing: money.

Fifty years from now, Dallas will be a cosmopolitan metropolis, home to a diverse population and a wide range of multinational corporations. But in 1963, the population of 747,000 is overwhelmingly white, 97 percent Protestant, and growing larger

Downtown Dallas. Reunion Tower rises above the city. The low, curved colonnade is in Dealey Plaza. [© Corbis]

Reverend Billy Graham was seated next to President Kennedy at a prayer breakfast in the Mayflower Hotel in Washington, D.C., in 1961. [JFK Presidential Library and Museum]

and more conservative by the day as newcomers flood in from rural Texas and Louisiana.

But most of all, Dallas is a city that does not trust outsiders or their political views, particularly those of liberal Yankees. John Kennedy has heard many negative reports about Dallas. Trusted friends are warning him to cancel this leg of his Texas trip. Senator J. William Fulbright of Arkansas confided to John Kennedy that he was physically afraid of entering Dallas, calling it "a very dangerous place."

"I wouldn't go there," he told JFK. "Don't you go."

Evangelist Billy Graham also warns the president to stay away. Texas congressman Ralph Yarborough's two brothers live and work in Dallas, and both make a point of telling him that the city hates Kennedy. And in early November, Byron Skelton of the Texas Democratic National Committee will have a premonition that JFK may be placing himself in grave danger by coming to Dallas. Skelton will repeatedly warn the president to stay away.

But John Kennedy is the president of the United States of America—all of them. There should be no place in this vast country where he has to be afraid to visit.

JFK has decided to visit Big D. There is no backing down.

CHAPTER TWENTY-SEVEN

NOVEMBER 1, 1963
Irving, Texas 2:30 P.M.

IT IS FRIDAY AFTERNOON, AND A WEARY James Hosty Jr. rings the bell at Ruth Paine's home. The burly 39-year-old FBI agent has spent the day investigating cases in nearby Fort Worth. He is juggling almost 40 investigations right now, taking small bites out of each one. But any case involving J. Edgar Hoover's battle against communism gets top priority, which is why Hosty is stopping at Mrs. Paine's rather than driving straight back into Dallas to start his weekend. The agent is looking for Lee Harvey Oswald. The bureau has received a tip from the CIA about Oswald's visit to the Cuban embassy in Mexico City in September, and agents are now anxious to find him.

Mrs. Paine opens the door. Hosty flashes his badge, explaining that he's a special agent of the FBI, and asks if they can talk.

Mrs. Paine is cordial to James Hosty. She invites him inside and says that this is the first time she's ever met an FBI agent.

Special Agent Hosty is the FBI's expert on Lee and Marina Oswald. Back in March, he opened a file on Marina in order to keep tabs on the Soviet citizen. Later that month, he requested that Lee's file be reopened due to Oswald's obvious communist sympathies. The agent has tracked the Oswalds from apartment to apartment, from Dallas to New Orleans and back again. But now the trail has grown cold.

Hosty asks Ruth Paine if she knows where he can find the man.

Paine acknowledges that Marina and her two girls live in her home. After a moment's hesitation, she admits that she doesn't know where Oswald lives, though she does know that he works at the Texas School Book Depository in downtown Dallas. Paine gets a phone book and looks up the address: 411 Elm Street.

Hosty writes all this down.

Ruth Paine. This photo was taken on December 5, 1963. [© Associated Press]

CHAPTER TWENTY-EIGHT

NOVEMBER 4, 1963

Washington, D.C.

SPECIAL AGENT WINSTON G. LAWSON of the Secret Service's White House detail is informed of the president's upcoming trip to Dallas.

Lawson, a Korean War veteran in his early 30s, specializes in planning Kennedy's official travels. As with all such visits, his primary responsibilities are to identify individuals who might be a threat to the president, take action against anyone considered to be such a threat, and plan security for the president's appearances and motorcade route.

There is still debate about whether there is to be a motorcade through downtown Dallas. Lawson knows that Dallas is a security nightmare because of the more than 20,000 windows lining the city's major streets. The more windows, the more places to hide a gunman aiming at the president's limousine.

But Lawson temporarily sets that question aside. He begins his investigation of potential threats by combing through the

Secret Service's Protective Research Section (PRS). These files list all individuals who have threatened the president or are potentially dangerous to him. A check of the PRS on November 8 by Lawson reveals that there are no potentially dangerous people in the Dallas area.

Lawson then travels to Texas and interviews local law enforcement and other federal agencies, continuing his search for individuals who might be a threat to John F. Kennedy. The FBI comes up with the name of a Dallas-area resident who might be a serious threat. But it is not the name of Lee Harvey Oswald. Instead, it is a known local troublemaker who has no plans to kill the president of the United States.

Special Agent Winston G. Lawson of the Secret Service White House detail. [JFK Presidential Library and Museum]

CHAPTER TWENTY-NINE

NOVEMBER 16, 1963

Dallas, Texas 1:50 P.M.

THIRTEEN-YEAR-OLD STERLING WOOD AIMS his Winchester .30-30 rifle at the silhouette of a man's head. He
exhales and squeezes the trigger, then squints downrange at the
target. It is Saturday. Sterling and his father, Homer, have come
to the Sports Drome Rifle Range to get their guns ready for
deer season.

The boy notices a young man standing in the shooting booth
next to him. He is aiming at a similar silhouette. The teenager
reads a lot of gun books and is pretty sure that the guy is firing
an Italian carbine. It appears that the rifle's barrel has been
sawed off to make it shorter, but it's still longer than Sterling's
Winchester by a few inches.

"Daddy," Sterling whispers to his father, "it looks like a 6.5
Italian carbine."

*This advertisement from a gun magazine shows the type of rifle
that Oswald ordered through the mail.* [© Bettmann/Corbis]

The man shoots. Flame leaps from the end of the gun because of its shortened length. Sterling can actually feel the heat from the blast. The gunman removes the spent cartridge and places it in his pocket as if he doesn't want to leave behind evidence that he's been there. Sterling finds it unusual that the shooter does this after each and every round.

The teenager is impressed that almost all the shooter's bullet holes are clustered around what would be the eye if the paper target were a real man.

Sterling will later testify that he believes this man is Lee Harvey Oswald.

———

Oswald turned 24 just a month ago. He has little to show for his time on earth. He is in an on-again, off-again relationship with his wife and children. He works a menial job. And despite his sharp intellect, he has no higher education. He doesn't know whether he wants to be an American, a Cuban, or a Russian.

Bullets like these were used in carbine rifles.
[© Blaz Kure/Shutterstock.com]

Still, he longs to be a great man—a significant man whose name will never be forgotten. And so far, the only person who seems to be impressed with him is the kid at the shooting range.

Marina Oswald with June on the left and Rachel in her lap. This photograph was taken two days after the assassination. [© Tom Dillard/Dallas Morning News/Corbis]

CHAPTER THIRTY

NOVEMBER 18, 1963
Dallas, Texas

SPECIAL AGENT WINSTON G. LAWSON, Forrest V. Sorrels of the Secret Service's Dallas office, and Dallas police chief Jesse Curry drive the proposed motorcade route from Love Field airport to the Dallas Trade Mart, a huge showroom building where the president is scheduled to give a lunch speech to 2,600 people. Special Agent Sorrels is very concerned about the many buildings and grass borders along the route. He will later testify that "during the time that we were making this survey with the police, I made the remark that if someone wanted to get the President of the United States, he could do it with a high-powered rifle and a telescopic sight from some building or some hillside."

Nevertheless, the agents decide that this will be the presidential motorcade route.

Anytime the president of the United States drives through a crowded city, there is a careful balance between protecting his

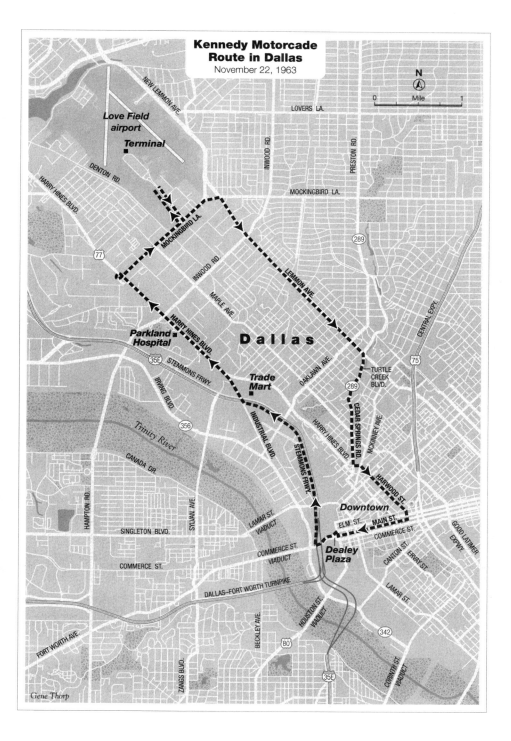

Kennedy Motorcade Route in Dallas
November 22, 1963

N

0   Mile   1

NEW LEMMON AVE.

LOVERS LA.

Love Field airport

Terminal

DENTON RD.

INWOOD RD.

PRESTON RD.

MOCKINGBIRD LA.

HARRY HINES BLVD.

77

MOCKINGBIRD LA.

INWOOD RD.

MAPLE AVE.

LEMMON AVE.

289

Dallas

CENTRAL EXPY.

Parkland Hospital

HARRY HINES BLVD.

35E   STEMMONS FRWY.

OAKLAWN AVE.

289

TURTLE CREEK BLVD.

75

IRVING BLVD.

Trade Mart

INDUSTRIAL BLVD.

HARRY HINES BLVD.

CEDAR SPRINGS RD.

McKINNEY AVE.

Trinity River

356

CANADA DR.

STEMMONS FRWY.

HARWOOD ST.

HAMPTON RD.

SINGLETON BLVD.

SYLVAN AVE.

LAMAR ST. VIADUCT

COMMERCE ST. VIADUCT

COMMERCE ST.

ELM ST.

Downtown

MAIN ST.

COMMERCE ST.

GOOD LATIMER EXPWY.

CANTON ST.

ERVAY ST.

LAMAR ST.

Dealey Plaza

DALLAS–FORT WORTH TURNPIKE

BECKLEY AVE.

HOUSTON ST. VIADUCT

342

FORT WORTH AVE.

ZANGS BLVD.

80

35E

CORINTH ST. VIADUCT

Gene Thorp

This photograph shows where Secret Service agents should be when the president is in a motorcade.
It was taken when Kennedy was in Cork, Ireland, in June 1963. [JFK Presidential Library and Museum]

life and ensuring that the maximum number of people can see the chief executive. A perfect motorcade route doesn't have high windows from which a sniper can poke a gun. It offers alternative routes in case something goes wrong, features wide streets that keep crowds far back from the vehicles, and has few, if any, tight turns.

The Dallas motorcade route violates each of these principles.

Secret Service agents are trained to position their bodies between the president and the crowd, acting as human shields. While doing so, they are supposed to study the area and look up at windows for signs of a gunman or rifle barrel. The president's limousine has running boards on both sides that allow the agents to shield the president while also performing this scan. They hold on to handles fixed to the car for balance. However, JFK does not like the agents to stand on the running boards because this blocks the crowd's view of him, so they often ride one car behind.

CHAPTER THIRTY-ONE

NOVEMBER 21, 1963

Aboard *Air Force One* 2:00 P.M.

TODAY'S JOURNEY BEGAN AT 9:15 A.M., when John Kennedy said good-bye to Caroline as she set off to the third floor of the White House for school. John Jr., who will be three years old next week, got the privilege of riding with his parents in the presidential helicopter from the White House to *Air Force One*. The young boy enjoyed the trip immensely.

But as *Marine One* set down on the runway next to the presidential plane, young John pleaded for his journey to continue. "I want to come," he said to his father.

"You can't," the president replied softly.

"It's just a few days," the first lady reminded the crying child. "And when we come back, it will be your birthday."

John Jr. began to sob. "John, like Mummy said, we'll be back in a few days," the president explained. JFK then kissed his son.

*The Kennedys at the White House
Christmas party, 1962.*

*Mrs. Kennedy hosts a tea for the wives of
new ambassadors, September 20, 1961.*

*JKF congratulates opera singer Grace Bumbry
after a performance at a White House dinner,
February 20, 1962.*

*The first lady during her official trip to India,
March 1962.*

The president and first lady, March 28, 1963.

Formal Life

Cellist Pablo Casals stands before the audience after a concert in the East Room, November 13, 1961.

The last photo of the Kennedy family, taken on the south balcony of the White House, as they watch the Royal Highland Regiment, November 13, 1963.

The Kennedys with Jawaharlal Nehru, prime minister of India, and his daughter Indira Gandhi before a dinner to honor Nehru, November 7, 1961.

The president at Veterans Day ceremonies in Arlington National Cemetery, November 11, 1961.

The Kennedys at Mount Vernon with Mohammad Ayub Khan, the president of Pakistan, and his daughter, Begum Nasir Akhtar Aurangzeb, July 11, 1961.

WHITE HOUSE ROOMS

The Red Room.

The Oval Office with JFK's favorite rocking chair.

Jacqueline Kennedy stands with members of the National Society of Interior Designers, who donated the antique wallpaper in the Diplomatic Reception Room.

State Dining Room before renovation.

State Dining Room after renovation with a new carpet.

WHITE HOUSE ROOMS

*The Lincoln Bedroom, with portraits
of Abraham Lincoln (left) and
Mary Todd Lincoln (right).*

The Green Room.

The East Room.

Jacqueline Kennedy's dressing room.

*Treaty Room, with portraits of presidents
Zachary Taylor (left) and
Andrew Johnson (right).*

FAMILY LIFE

Leaving church after Mass.

Caroline Kennedy.

A Christmas bow.

The family at Camp David, the
presidential weekend home in Maryland.
Caroline sits on Macaroni.

FAMILY LIFE

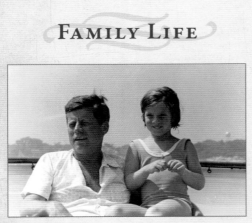

The president and his daughter on vacation.

John Jr. steers the boat.

*Caroline gets a lift across
the White House lawn.*

A family vacation on Squaw Island, Massachusetts, with many dogs.

FAMILY LIFE

Playing hide-and-seek with the president of the United States.

Picnicking on the White House lawn.

Jacqueline greets Sardar, a gift from the president of Pakistan.

Caroline and John Jr. ready for Halloween, 1963.

FIRST PETS

John Jr. and Shannon.

Charlie.

Clipper.

Pushinka and her puppies.

The Kennedy home was filled with pets.
The family also had Debbie and Billie,
hamsters; Tom Kitten, a gray cat; Robin,
a canary; Maybelle and Bluebell, parakeets;
Wolf, an Irish wolfhound; and Tex, a pony.

Caroline and Macaroni.

All images in this insert courtesy of JKF Presidential Library and Museum.

A U.S. Army helicopter often transports the president and his family to airports or other destinations close to Washington, D.C. [JFK Presidential Library and Museum]

*Caroline Kennedy grins at White House photographer
Cecil Stoughton. Secret Service agent Robert Foster sits
next to her.* [JFK Presidential Library and Museum]

Turning toward the Secret Service agent in charge of the boy's protection: "You take care of John for me, Mr. Foster," he ordered gently.

At 11:00 A.M., the president gave John Jr. one last hug and stepped onto the tarmac before climbing the steps up into *Air Force One*. The first lady was at his side.

Five minutes later, the plane went wheels-up for the three-and-a-half-hour flight to Texas. John Kennedy Jr. watched the great jet rise into the sky and disappear into the distance.

President John F. Kennedy pored over the "Eyes Only, President" intelligence documents overflowing from his battered black briefcase.

Air Force One will land first in San Antonio. Then on to Houston and then Fort Worth, where the president and first lady will spend the night. Dallas will come tomorrow. JFK's personal pilot, Colonel Jim Swindal, will take the Kennedys from Fort Worth into Dallas's Love Field. The flight will be short, just 13 minutes. But

Air Force One, *a specially fitted Boeing 707, was called the*
flying White House. [JFK Presidential Library and Museum]

the symbolic image of *Air Force One* descending from the heavens to land in that troubled city will be a far more powerful sight than John Kennedy driving 35 miles across the prairie in a limousine.

JFK gets up and makes his way back to the first family's quarters. He taps lightly on the door and pokes his head in. "You all right?" he asks Jackie. They will be landing soon. "Fine," the first lady responds.

"I just wanted to be sure," he tells her, closing the door.

The president feels a slight dip as *Air Force One* begins to descend. He looks out the window. Five miles below and slowly rising up to greet him is the barren and flat landscape of Texas.

On the ground in Dallas, Lee Harvey Oswald stuffs cardboard shipping boxes with books as he fills orders at the Texas School

Book Depository. But today he is easily distracted. A map of the motorcade route was printed on the front page of the *Dallas Times Herald*'s afternoon edition and caught his attention. *Air Force One* will land at Love Field, and from there, the president will travel to the Trade Mart to give a speech. On the way, he will pass the Texas School Book Depository.

Oswald looks out the nearest window and sees precisely where President Kennedy's limousine will make a slow right turn from Main Street onto Houston, then an even slower left-hand turn onto Elm, where it will pass almost directly below the windows of the depository. Getting a good glimpse of the president will be as simple as looking down onto the street below.

But Lee Harvey Oswald is planning to do much more than catch a glimpse. In fact, he is quietly plotting to shoot the president. Oswald does not hate the president. He has no reason to want JFK

dead. He is, however, bitter that a man such as John Kennedy has so many advantages in life. Oswald well understands that it's easier for men born into privilege

Several views of the sixth floor taken on November 22, 1963.
[NARA/JFK Assassination Records]

Investigators carry the container made of paper that Oswald used to hide his rifle. It was found on the sixth floor of the Texas School Book Depository building after the assassination. [© Bettmann/Corbis]

to distinguish themselves. But other than that small amount of envy, he does not speak unfavorably about the president. In fact, Oswald wants to be like JFK.

Above all, he wants to be a great man.

⎯⎯⎯⎯

"Can I ride home with you this afternoon?" Oswald casually asks Wesley Frazier. His 19-year-old co-worker's home is in the suburb of Irving, a half block from where Marina Oswald lives with Ruth Paine. Oswald often catches a ride out there on Fridays.

But then Frazier realizes that today isn't Friday. It's Thursday—and Oswald never rides to Irving on Thursdays. "Why are you going home today?" Frazier asks him.

"I am going home to get some curtain rods," Oswald replies.

Oswald then steals a length of brown wrapping paper from the depository's shipping department. He spends the rest of his work-day making a bag in which to conceal his rifle.

CHAPTER THIRTY-TWO

NOVEMBER 22, 1963

Fort Worth, Texas 7:30 A.M.

"IT'S RAINING," SAYS GEORGE THOMAS, stepping inside John Kennedy's Fort Worth hotel suite. The president's valet wakes him up at 7:30 A.M. A crowd is already gathering in the parking lot eight floors below, waiting to hear Kennedy speak to them from the back of a flatbed truck. The audience of nearly 5,000 is mostly male union workers. Many have been standing in the rain for hours.

"That's too bad," Kennedy replies to his valet. Rain means that the bubble-top roof will be buckled onto his limousine for the Dallas motorcade. Not only will the local citizens be upset by having to wait in the cold and rain for hours until he passes by, but their inability to get a clear glimpse of the president and first lady inside the bubble will do little to secure their votes next November.

The president wraps himself in his back brace, tightly adjusting the straps. He then dresses in a blue suit, a dark blue tie, and a white shirt with gray stripes. He reads the CIA situation reports and scans several newspapers. The *Chicago Sun-Times* is reporting that Jackie just might be the pivotal factor in helping him get re-elected in 1964. That's the best news of this trip so far: Everyone loves the first lady. The people of Texas screamed and cheered for

Kennedy speaks to the crowd from a decorated truck flatbed outside his hotel. [JFK Presidential Library and Museum]

JFK on the first day of the Texas trip. But as big as his ovations are, and as intently as the audiences hang on every word of his speeches, the receptions John Kennedy receives are nothing like what his wife is experiencing. Jackie is the talk of Texas, and bringing her along may just be the smartest political move the president has ever made.

By 9:00 A.M., John Kennedy is standing on the back of the flatbed truck, looking upbeat and triumphant. "There are no faint hearts in Forth Worth," he says approvingly to the crowd. He has a well-deserved reputation for not giving in to the elements. The union workers knew their waiting in the rain would be rewarded and that the speech would not be canceled.

"Where's Jackie?" someone shouts.

"Where's Jackie?" yells another voice.

John Kennedy smiles and points up to her hotel room. "Mrs. Kennedy is organizing herself," he jokes. "It takes longer," the president adds. "But, of course, she looks better than we do when she does it."

The crowd roars in laughter.

The energy in the Fort Worth parking lot fuels the president, who delivers a powerful and impassioned speech. "We are going forward!" he exclaims in closing, reminding his audience that he is keeping the promises he made in his inaugural address less than three years earlier.

Next page: *Kennedy pushes into the crowd in Fort Worth, Texas, November 22, 1963.* [JFK Presidential Library and Museum]

The earsplitting cries of approval from those thousands of hardened union men is all the proof John Kennedy needs that Texas really isn't such a bad place after all.

The president rides a wave of adrenaline off the stage and back into the hotel. Campaigning revitalizes him, even in an early-morning Texas drizzle.

But as good as he feels, the president knows that the rest of Friday, November 22, is not going to be easy. From both a political and a personal standpoint, he must be at the top of his game if he is going to win over the hardened people of Dallas.

President Kennedy and Jackie leave their Fort Worth hotel on the way to the airport for the short flight to Dallas. [JFK Presidential Library and Museum]

CHAPTER THIRTY-THREE

NOVEMBER 22, 1963

Dallas, Texas 7:55 A.M.

O SWALD AND WESLEY FRAZIER ARE PULLING UP for work at the Texas School Book Depository. Oswald, leaping out of the car as Frazier cuts the engine, grabs his brown package and races inside the building before Frazier can catch up and ask him why he's in such a hurry.

9:45 A.M.

Crowds of eager Dallas residents stand on the curb in front of the Texas School Book Depository. The president won't pass by for three hours, but they've come early to get a good spot. Best of all, it looks like the sun might come out. Maybe they'll get a good glimpse of John F. Kennedy and Jackie after all.

Lee Harvey Oswald peers out a first-floor window of the depository building, assessing the president's route by where the crowds stand. He can clearly see the corner of Elm and Houston, where John Kennedy's limousine will make a slow left turn.

A modern photograph looking out the sixth-floor window of the Texas School Book Depository. The tall building in the background is Reunion Tower. [LOC, HS 503-3330]

This is important to Oswald. He's selected a spot on the depository's sixth floor as his sniper's roost. Stacks of book boxes near the window overlooking Elm and Houston form a natural hiding place, allowing Oswald to poke his rifle outside and sight the motorcade as it makes that deliberate turn. The marksman in Lee Harvey Oswald knows that he'll have time for two shots, maybe even three if he works quickly enough.

But one should be all he needs.

Kennedy shakes hands with Colonel Jim Swindal at his promotion in 1962. Swindal is the pilot of Air Force One. [JFK Presidential Library and Museum]

11:35 A.M.
Colonel Jim Swindal eases *Air Force One* down onto the runway at Love Field. John Kennedy is optimistic. Peering out the windows of his airplane, he sees that the weather has turned sunny and warm and another large Texas crowd is waiting to greet him. "This trip is turning out to be terrific,"

he happily confides to Kenny O'Donnell. "Here we are in Dallas, and it looks like everything in Texas will turn out to be fine for us!"

Police cars circle the field, and officers are stationed on rooftops. But these are the only ominous sights at the airport. The welcoming party of about 2,000 are overjoyed to see *Air Force One* touch down, marking the first time a president has visited Dallas since 1948. Texans Vice President Lyndon Johnson and his wife, Claudia, who is called Lady Bird, wait on the tarmac to greet the president. Jackie emerges from the rear door of the plane, radiant in her pink Chanel suit with the matching pillbox hat. Two steps behind comes John Kennedy.

"I can see his suntan all the way from here!" the local TV reporter gushes.

President Kennedy and Jackie Kennedy arrive in Dallas, Texas.
[JFK Presidential Library and Museum]

A large crowd was waiting at Love Field. The president once again spent time shaking hands and signing autographs. [JFK Presidential Library and Museum]

The official plan is for JFK to head straight for his limousine to join the motorcade, but instead he breaks off and heads into the crowd. Not content with merely shaking a few hands, the president pushes deep into the throng, dragging Jackie along with him. The two of them remain surrounded by this wall of people for more than a full minute, much to the crowd's delight. Then the president and first lady reemerge, only to wade deep into another section of crowd.

"Boy, this is something," says the local reporter. "This is a bonus for the people who have waited out here!"

The president and first lady shake hands for what seems like an eternity to their very nervous Secret Service detail. "Kennedy is showing he is not afraid," Ronnie Dugger of the *Texas Observer* writes in his notebook.

Finally, John and Jackie Kennedy make their way to the presidential limousine. Governor John Connally and his wife, Nellie, are waiting for them in the car. There are three rows of seats in the vehicle. Up front is the driver, 54-year-old Bill Greer. To his right sits Roy Kellerman—like Greer, a longtime Secret Service agent. Special Agent Kellerman has served on the White House detail since the early days of World War II and has protected presidents Roosevelt, Truman, Eisenhower, and now Kennedy.

JFK sits in the back seat. Jackie sits to his left. The first lady was handed a bouquet of red roses upon landing in Dallas, and these now rest on the seat between her and the president.

Governor Connally sits directly in front of the president, in the

middle row, known as jump seats. Connally takes off his 10-gallon hat so that the crowds can see him. Nellie sits in front of Jackie and right behind the driver.

11:55 A.M.

As the motorcade leaves Love Field, the presidential limousine—Secret Service code name SS-100-X—is the second car in line, flanked on either side by four motorcycle escorts. Up front is an advance car with local police and Secret Service, among them Dallas police chief Jesse Curry and Secret Service special agent Winston Lawson.

Behind John Kennedy's vehicle is a follow-up convertible code-named Halfback. Dave Powers and Kenny O'Donnell sit here, surrounded by Secret Service agents heavily armed with handguns and automatic weapons. Clint Hill, head of the first lady's Secret Service detail, stands on the left running board of Halfback. Special agents Bill McIntyre, John Ready, and Paul Landis also man the running boards.

The president with Jackie seated behind Texas governor John Connally and his wife, Nellie. [LOC, USZ62-134844]

Car four is a convertible limousine that has been rented locally for the vice president. Bringing up the rear is car five, code-named Varsity and occupied by a Texas state policeman and four Secret Service agents.

Way up at the front of the motorcade, driving several car lengths in front of SS-100-X, Dallas police chief Jesse Curry is committed to making the president's visit as incident-free as possible. Curry has been involved in almost every aspect of the planning for John Kennedy's visit and is dedicating 350 men—a full third of his force—to lining the motorcade route, handling security for the president's airport arrival, and policing the crowd at the Trade Mart speech.

Curry has ordered his men to face toward the street, rather than toward the crowd, thinking it wouldn't hurt for them to see the man they're protecting as a reward for the long hours they will be on their feet. But this means that the policemen won't be helping the Secret Service protect the president by scanning the city's many windows for signs of a sniper's rifle. And Curry has chosen not to position any men in the vicinity of Dealey Plaza, thinking that most of the crowds will gather before that spot.

Crowds greet the presidential motorcade. The Secret Service ride in the car behind the president's limousine. [© Associated Press]

NOVEMBER 22, 1963

Dallas, Texas Noon

I T'S LUNCHTIME AT THE Texas School Book Depository. Most of Lee Harvey Oswald's coworkers have left the building, hoping to get a glimpse of the president, so the sixth floor is deserted.

Just down the block, FBI special agent James Hosty has forgotten all about investigating Lee Harvey Oswald and is just trying to make sure he gets a look at his hero, President Kennedy.

Lee Harvey Oswald didn't bring a lunch to work today. And he doesn't plan on eating. Instead, he gets into position at the window behind the boxes of books.

At 12:24 P.M., nearly 30 minutes into the motorcade, the president's car passes Special Agent James Hosty on the corner of Main Street and Field. Hosty gets his wish and sees Kennedy in the flesh, before turning back around and walking into the Alamo Grill for lunch.

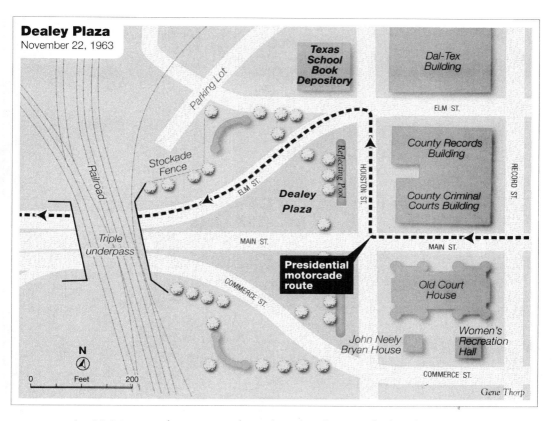

Texas
School
Book
Depository

Dal-Tex
Building

ELM ST.

Parking Lot

Stockade
Fence

Railroad

Reflecting Pool

ELM ST.

*Dealey
Plaza*

HOUSTON ST.

County Records
Building

RECORD ST.

County Criminal
Courts Building

Triple
underpass

MAIN ST.

MAIN ST.

**Presidential
motorcade
route**

COMMERCE ST.

Old Court
House

John Neely
Bryan House

Women's
Recreation
Hall

COMMERCE ST.

N

0   Feet   200

Gene Thorp

At 12:29 P.M., the motorcade makes the sharp right-hand turn onto Houston Street. From high above, in his sixth-floor sniper's lair, Lee Harvey Oswald sees John F. Kennedy in person for the first time. He quickly sights his Italian carbine, taking aim through the scope as the motorcade skirts the edge of Dealey Plaza.

The crowds here are still large and enthusiastic, despite Chief Curry's prediction that they would have thinned out by this point. The people shout for Jackie and the president to look their way. As they have agreed, JFK waves at the people standing in front of

buildings on the right side of the road, while Jackie waves at those standing along grassy Dealey Plaza, to their left. This ensures that no voter goes without a wave.

The motorcade is just five minutes from the Trade Mart, where Kennedy will make his speech. Almost there.

Inside the presidential limousine, Nellie Connally stops waving long enough to look over her right shoulder and smile at John Kennedy. "Mr. President, you can't say Dallas doesn't love you."

At that very moment, if JFK had looked up to the sixth floor of the Texas School Book Depository, he would have seen a rifle barrel sticking out of an open window, pointed directly at his head.

But Kennedy doesn't look up.

Nor does the Secret Service.

For most of the trip, Kennedy and Jackie shared smiles on their side of the road.
[© Bettmann/Corbis]

It is 12:30 P.M. The time has come for Special Agent Bill Greer to steer the limousine through the sweeping 120-degree left turn from Houston and onto Elm.

———◆———

Lee Harvey Oswald leans hard against the left window and presses the butt of the Mannlicher-Carcano against his right shoulder. The scratched wooden stock of the gun rests against his cheek. His right index finger is curled around the trigger.

He peers into his telescopic sight. John Kennedy's head looks as if it is two feet away. Oswald knows time is short. He'll be able to shoot two shots for sure. Three if he's quick. He probably has only nine seconds.

Seeing his target clearly, Oswald exhales, gently squeezes the trigger, and even as he feels the recoil kick the rifle hard against his shoulder, he smoothly pulls back the bolt to chamber another round. He can't tell whether the first bullet has done much damage. But that doesn't matter. Oswald must immediately fire again.

Because if the first shot somehow misses, just like that shot missed General Walker back in April, and the president lives, Oswald will look like a fool again. And that's the last thing he wants. No, the plan is to kill John Fitzgerald Kennedy. And Lee Harvey Oswald will see that plan through.

He doesn't think twice. Oswald fires again.

The sound of the second shot is so loud that pieces of the plaster ceiling inside the Texas School Book Depository fall and the panes of the windows Lee Harvey Oswald stands next to rattle.

Approximately 8.4 seconds after firing his first shot, Lee Harvey Oswald pulls the trigger a third time. And then Oswald bolts. He drops the gun, steps out from the tower of boxes, and runs down the stairs.

Upon hearing the first shot, Dallas motorcycle officer Marrion Baker raced into the building and up the stairs. He stops Oswald at gunpoint on the second floor but lets him go when it becomes clear that Oswald is an employee.

Sixty seconds later, the 24-year-old assassin walks out into the sunshine.

Photograph of the sixth floor of the Texas School Book Depository taken on November 22, 1963. Oswald stood at the window on the right, behind the stacks of boxes. [NARA/JFK Assassination Records]

CHAPTER THIRTY-FIVE

NOVEMBER 22, 1963

Dallas, Texas 12:30 P.M.

EARWITNESS TESTIMONY IN DEALEY PLAZA will later confirm that three shots were fired from the depository. One of the shots misses the president's car completely, and decades later, people still wonder whether it was the first or third shot. But the fact remains that two of the shots did not miss.

The first impact strikes the president in the back of his lower neck. Traveling at 1,904 feet per second, the 6.5-millimeter round tears through the president's trachea and then exits his body through the tight knot of his dark blue tie. No bones are struck, and though his right lung is bruised, JFK's heart and lungs still function perfectly.

The president is badly hurt, but very much alive. He has trouble breathing and talking as blood floods into his windpipe. Otherwise, the rifle shot will most likely not kill him.

The same cannot be said for Texas governor John Connally. His jump seat, immediately in front of the president, is three inches lower than where the president is currently sitting. Ballistic studies performed later show that the bullet passed through Kennedy, then entered Connally's back.

The governor had turned his body just before Oswald fired the shot. He was twisting around, trying to speak face-to-face with the president. The bullet pierces Connally's skin and travels through his body, exiting below the right side of his chest. But it isn't finished. It then pierces the governor's wrist and deflects off the bones and into his left thigh, where it finally comes to rest.

The blow knocks Governor Connally forward, bending him double. His chest is immediately drenched in blood. "No, no, no, no," he cries, "they're going to kill us all."

Roy Kellerman thinks he hears the president yell, "My God,

People take cover after they hear gunshots. [© Bettmann/Corbis]

I'm hit," and turns to look over his left shoulder at the man whose Boston accent he knows so well.

Kellerman sees that JFK has been shot.

The torso of a normal man would have been shoved farther forward by the force of a bullet striking his body at nearly twice the

Clint Hill climbs onto the trunk of the presidential limousine. [© Bettmann/Corbis]

speed of sound. This is precisely what happened to Governor Connally. If John F. Kennedy had been knocked forward, he might have lived a long life.

But now the president's painful struggle with back problems returns to torture him one last time. The back brace that he is wearing holds his body straight up. If not for the brace, the next bullet, fired less than five seconds later, would have traveled harmlessly over his head.

But it does not. The next bullet explodes his skull.

The diameter of the entry wound from the second impact is just slightly wider than that of a number two pencil. The bullet barely slows as it slices through the tender gray brain matter before exploding out of the front of his head. This bullet ends John F. Kennedy's life in an instant.

Secret Service special agent Clint Hill hears the shots and leaps into action. Shoving himself away from the running board on Halfback, the vehicle directly behind the president's limousine, Hill sprints forward in an effort to jump on the small step that sticks out from the back of the president's car.

Meanwhile, JFK is leaning to his left, but still upright. Jackie wraps her hands lovingly around her husband's face.

Jackie's arms are still wrapped around her husband when the front of his head explodes. Brains, blood, and bone fragments shower the first lady's face and clothes. The matter sprays as far forward as the limousine's windshield visors.

The man who swam miles to save the men of *PT-109*, who has

shaken the hands of kings and queens and prime ministers, who inspired the entire world with his bold speeches and deeply held belief in the power of democracy and freedom, who caressed the cheeks of his children, who endured the loss of loved ones, and who stood toe-to-toe with men who might otherwise have destroyed the world, is brain dead.

Jackie leans toward JFK. This photograph was taken by a witness, Mary Moorman, a fraction of a second after the first shot. [© Corbis]

CHAPTER THIRTY-SIX

NOVEMBER 22, 1963

Dallas, Texas 12:31 P.M.

INSIDE THE PRESIDENTIAL LIMOUSINE, there is chaos.

"Oh, no, no, no. Oh, my God. They have shot my husband. I love you, Jack," Jackie Kennedy cries.

Up front, driver Bill Greer and Special Agent Roy Kellerman are radioing that the president has been hit. Bill Greer speeds toward nearby Parkland Hospital with the accelerator all the way to the floor.

The president's body falls over and onto Jackie's lap. She holds his head in her white-gloved hands,

The presidential limousine with its trunk open parked at the emergency entrance at Parkland Hospital.
[Tom Dillard/Dallas Morning News/Corbis]

cradling him as if he has simply fallen asleep. "Jack, Jack. What have they done to you?"

———

The radio call of "Code 3" means an emergency of the highest importance to Dallas-area hospitals. The term is almost never used. So when Parkland dispatcher Anne Ferguson requests more details, she is simply told, "The president has been shot."

The time is 12:33 P.M.

Three minutes later, the presidential limousine roars into Parkland, blowing past the sign reading EMERGENCY CASES ONLY. Bill Greer parks in the middle of the three ambulance bays.

But there is no stretcher waiting, no emergency team waiting to help the president. Incredibly, there has been a breakdown in communications. The trauma team has just been notified.

Jackie Kennedy refuses to let go of her husband. The first lady curls her body forward around the president's blood-soaked face.

"Mrs. Kennedy," Special Agent Clint Hill says, "please let us help the president."

Jackie doesn't respond.

Hill realizes something. It's bad enough that she is seeing the man she loves with his head blown apart, but she doesn't want anyone else seeing him like that. There is no way in the world Jackie will allow John Fitzgerald Kennedy to be photographed in this state.

A crowd gathers at Parkland Hospital, anxiously waiting for news of the president's condition. [© Bettmann/Corbis]

Knowing in an instant that it is the right thing to do, Special Agent Hill removes his suit coat and sets it gently atop the president's body. Jackie Kennedy wraps her husband's head and shoulders in Clint Hill's coat.

The president is placed on a gurney and hustled into the hospital and down the corridor to Trauma Room One.

An overhead fluorescent lamp lights the small army of medical professionals at work. A tube is inserted into John Kennedy's throat to open his airway, and to replace fluids, saline solution is pumped into his body through a vein in his thigh.

The room slowly fills with surgeons, until there are 14 doctors standing over the president. Outside the trauma room, Jackie rises from her chair, determined to enter. She has heard the talk about fluids and resuscitation and is beginning to hope that her husband just might live. A nurse blocks her path, but the gracious first lady can display an iron will when she wants to. "I'm going to get into that room," she repeats.

The first lady stands in a corner, out of the way, just wanting to be near her husband. Finally, Dr. William Kemp Clark, Parkland's chief neurosurgeon, knows they can do no more. A sheet is drawn over JFK's face. Dr. Clark turns to Jackie Kennedy. "Your husband has sustained a fatal wound," the veteran surgeon tells the first lady.

"I know," she replies.

"The president is dead."

Jackie leans up and presses her cheek to that of Dr. Clark. It is an expression of thanks. Dr. Clark, a hard man who served in the Pacific in World War II, can't help himself. He breaks down and sobs.

People burst into tears when hearing of Kennedy's death. [© Associated Press]

CHAPTER THIRTY-SEVEN

NOVEMBER 22, 1963
Dallas, Texas 1 P.M.

VICE PRESIDENT LYNDON JOHNSON is under constant watch from the instant his motorcade limousine arrives at Parkland Hospital. He is hustled into a small white cubicle in Parkland's Minor Medicine section with his wife, Lady Bird. A Secret Service detail guards his life. A patient and a nurse are kicked out to make room for them. The Secret Service wants LBJ flown immediately back to Washington and out of harm's way. Failing that, it would like him relocated to the safest possible security zone in Dallas: *Air Force One.*

But Vice President Johnson refuses to leave the hospital. He remains, waiting for word of President Kennedy's fate. The Secret Service pressures him again and again to depart, but LBJ will not go.

Shortly after 1:00 P.M., Kenny O'Donnell marches into the cubicle and stands before Lyndon Johnson. O'Donnell is openly distraught. He is not the sort of man who weeps at calamity, but the devastated look on his face is clear for all to see.

Even before O'Donnell opens his mouth, LBJ knows that it is official: Lyndon Baines Johnson is now the 36th president of the United States.

LBJ leaving Parkland Hospital after President Kennedy's death. His Secret Service agent, Rufus Youngblood, is in front of him and Representative Homer Thornberry from Texas follows. [© Bettmann/Corbis]

Bobby Kennedy gets the bad news from J. Edgar Hoover.

As the head of America's top law enforcement agency, Hoover is informed of the shooting almost immediately. The FBI director is a reserved man, but never more so than right now. He sits at his desk on the fifth floor of the Justice Department Building and picks up the phone to call Bobby Kennedy. It has been 15 minutes since Lee Harvey Oswald first pulled the trigger. The surgical trauma team at Parkland is fighting to keep the president alive.

Bobby is just about to eat a tuna fish sandwich on the patio of his Virginia home when his wife, Ethel, tells him he has a call.

"It's J. Edgar Hoover," she tells Bobby.

The attorney general knows this must be important. Hoover knows better than to call Bobby at home. He sets down his sandwich and goes to the phone. It's a special direct government line known as Extension 163.

"I have news for you," Hoover says. "The president has been shot."

Bobby hangs up. His first reaction is one of great distress, and his body seems to go slack. He answers phone call after phone call from friends and family. He holds back tears, but Ethel knows that her husband is breaking down and hands him a pair of dark glasses to hide his red-rimmed eyes.

⸺※⸺

Most people in the United States get the bad news from CBS newsman Walter Cronkite. He is called "the most trusted man in America" because of his simple, straightforward way of explaining world events.

Cronkite first breaks into the soap opera *As the World Turns* just eight minutes after the shooting, saying that an assassin has fired three shots at the president. Despite the fact that most Americans are at work or school, and not home watching daytime television, more than 75 million people are aware of the shooting by 2:00 P.M.

CBS newsman Walter Cronkite relays the news of Kennedy's death to the nation: "From Dallas, Texas, the flash—apparently official—President Kennedy died at 1:00 p.m. Central Standard Time, 2:00 p.m. Eastern Standard Time, some 38 minutes ago." [© CBS Photo Archive/Getty]

CHAPTER THIRTY-EIGHT

NOVEMBER 22, 1963

Dallas, Texas 12:33 P.M. to 1:50 P.M.

A LOT HAPPENS TO LEE HARVEY OSWALD between 12:30 P.M. and 1:00 P.M., but not what he expects. Nobody seems remotely interested in him.

Once out the door of the Texas School Book Depository, he walks east up Elm Street to catch a bus. The panic and chaos in Dealey Plaza recede behind him.

His escape plan is coming together slowly. For now, the assassin is on his way to his rooming house to pick up his pistol—just in case.

After his bus stalls in heavy post-assassination traffic, he gets off and walks a bit before finding a cab, which takes him closer to his rooming house at 1026 North Beckley. Upon arriving there, he races to his room, grabs his .38-caliber pistol, and sticks it in his waistband. Then he quickly leaves.

Little does Oswald know, but eyewitnesses at the scene have given the police his description. Now the police are on the

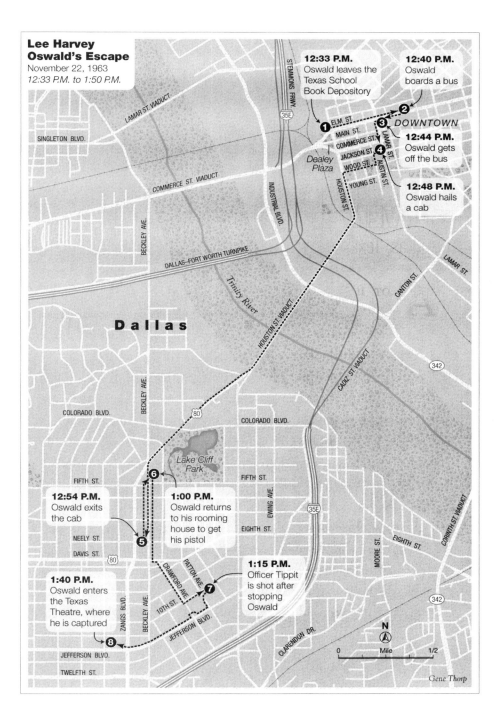

Lee Harvey Oswald's Escape
November 22, 1963
12:33 P.M. to 1:50 P.M.

12:33 P.M.
Oswald leaves the Texas School Book Depository

12:40 P.M.
Oswald boards a bus

12:44 P.M.
Oswald gets off the bus

12:48 P.M.
Oswald hails a cab

12:54 P.M.
Oswald exits the cab

1:00 P.M.
Oswald returns to his rooming house to get his pistol

1:15 P.M.
Officer Tippit is shot after stopping Oswald

1:40 P.M.
Oswald enters the Texas Theatre, where he is captured

D a l l a s

DOWNTOWN

Dealey Plaza

Lake Cliff Park

Trinity River

LAMAR ST. VIADUCT

SINGLETON BLVD.

STEMMONS FRWY.

35E

ELM ST.
MAIN ST.
COMMERCE ST.
JACKSON ST.
WOOD ST.
YOUNG ST.

LAMAR ST.
AUSTIN ST.

HOUSTON ST.

COMMERCE ST. VIADUCT

INDUSTRIAL BLVD.

BECKLEY AVE.

DALLAS–FORT WORTH TURNPIKE

HOUSTON ST. VIADUCT

CADIZ ST. VIADUCT

CANTON ST.

LAMAR ST.

342

COLORADO BLVD.

BECKLEY AVE.

80

COLORADO BLVD.

FIFTH ST.

FIFTH ST.

EWING AVE.

35E

NEELY ST.

DAVIS ST.

80

EIGHTH ST.

EIGHTH ST.

MOORE ST.

CORINTH ST. VIADUCT

CRAWFORD AVE.

PATTON AVE.

ZANGS BLVD.

BECKLEY AVE.

10TH ST.

JEFFERSON BLVD.

CLARENDON DR.

342

JEFFERSON BLVD.

TWELFTH ST.

N

0   Mile   1/2

Gene Thorp

Officer J. D. Tippit heard a description of the suspected assassin on the radio. Soon after, he saw Oswald and stopped him. This is a portrait painted from a photograph. [LOC, USZ62-132903]

lookout for a "white male, approximately 30, slender build, height 5 foot 10 inches, weight 165 pounds."

At 1:15 P.M., Officer J. D. Tippit of the Dallas Police Department is driving east on Tenth Street. Just after the intersection of Tenth and Patton, he sees a man matching the suspect's description wearing a light-colored jacket, walking alone.

Tippit pulls his car alongside Lee Harvey Oswald. He knows to be cautious; he has been with the Dallas Police Department for 11 years. But he also knows to be thorough in his questioning.

Oswald leans down and speaks to Tippit through the right front window vent. He is hostile. Tippit opens the door and steps out of his police cruiser. He walks to the front of the car, intending to ask Oswald a few more questions. Based on the answers, Tippit will then make a decision whether to place Oswald in handcuffs. But the policeman doesn't get farther than the front wheel. Lee Harvey Oswald pulls out his .38 and fires four bullets in rapid succession. Tippit is killed instantly.

Oswald, the man who nervously missed General Walker months ago, has now killed the president of the United States and a Dallas police officer in cold blood just 45 minutes apart.

But Oswald is running out of options. He has no money and very little ammunition, and the Dallas police know what he looks like. He will have to be very clever in these next few minutes if he is to make his escape.

The killer quickly reloads and continues his journey, turning down Patton Avenue. But this time he doesn't walk; he jogs. There is no doubt about it: Oswald is being hunted. The police are closing in. He needs to move quickly now. The time is 1:16 P.M.

Lee Harvey Oswald hears sirens and knows they're coming for him. He races toward the nearest hiding place he can find, a movie house called the Texas Theatre. Oswald has traveled eight blocks in the 25 minutes since killing Officer Tippit. He shed his jacket shortly after shooting Tippit, hoping to confuse his pursuers. He

The Texas Theatre as it appeared in 2009. [Courtesy of Andreas Praefcke/Wikicommons]

runs past the Bethel Temple, where a sign advises "Prepare to Meet Thy God."

But Lee Harvey Oswald is not showing fear. Foolishly, he runs right past the ticket booth. In the dark of the theater, he finds a seat, trying to make himself invisible.

After seeing the man run inside without paying, and at the same time hearing sirens as police cars race to the scene of Officer Tippit's murder, ticket taker Julia Postal puts two and two together. Realizing that the man she just saw is "running from them for some reason," she picks up the phone and dials the police.

Squad cars are on the scene almost immediately. Police close off

the theater's exits. The house lights are turned on. Patrolman M. N. McDonald approaches Oswald, who suddenly stands and punches the policeman in the face while reaching for the pistol in his waistband. McDonald is not hurt and immediately fights back. Other policemen join in. Finally, Lee Harvey Oswald is dragged out of the theater and taken to jail.

Police remove a rifle from the Texas School Depository on November 22, 1963. [© Corbis]

CHAPTER THIRTY-NINE

NOVEMBER 22, 1963

Air Force One   1:26 P.M. to 6:00 P.M.

AT 1:26 P.M. THE SECRET SERVICE WHISKS Lyndon Johnson to *Air Force One*, where he immediately climbs the steps up to the back door and waits for Jackie Kennedy to return to the plane. She has remained behind at Parkland, refusing to leave until the body of her husband comes with her.

They load the body onto *Air Force One* through the same rear door John Kennedy stepped out of three hours earlier. Jackie Kennedy waits until her husband's body is aboard before climbing up the steps. The inside of *Air Force One* is like an oven; the air-conditioning has been off for hours. The blinds are down, and the cabin is dark, out of fear that more assassins are on the loose and will shoot through the plane's windows. Yet Lyndon Johnson insists on being sworn in before *Air Force One* leaves the ground. Federal judge Sarah Hughes, who was personally appointed to the bench by LBJ, has been hastily

The casket holding the president's body is loaded onto Air Force One. [JFK Presidential Library and Museum]

Jackie Kennedy follows the casket on board. [JFK Presidential Library and Museum]

summoned to the presidential jet. She administers the oath of office of the president of the United States.

"You, Lyndon Baines Johnson, do solemnly swear . . ."

"I, Lyndon Baines Johnson, do solemnly swear . . ."

LBJ stands tall in *Air Force One.* To his left, still wearing the bloodstained pink suit, is Jacqueline Kennedy. The former first lady has not changed clothes. She is adamant that the world have a visual reminder of what happened to her husband here. Standing before Johnson is the judge.

Several feet behind them, in the rear of the plane, lies the body of

Lyndon Baines Johnson is sworn in as the 36th president of the United States, with his wife,
Lady Bird, on one side of him and Jackie Kennedy on the other. He placed his hand on a missal found
in Kennedy's bedroom on the plane. [JFK Presidential Library and Museum]

President Johnson addresses the nation live from Andrews Air Force Base in Maryland.
"This is a sad time for all people. We have suffered a loss that cannot be weighed."
[JFK Presidential Library and Museum]

John F. Kennedy. After the swearing-in ceremony, Jackie sits down in a seat next to the casket as the long ride home begins.

At 6:00 P.M. people are glued to their televisions with depressed fascination. It seems as if everyone finds out what is happening at the same time. People watch news anchors answer phones and read notes handed to them as events unfold.

The plane carrying John Kennedy's body touches down at

Bobby Kennedy and Jackie Kennedy watch as the president's coffin is moved from Air Force One *to an ambulance at Andrews Air Force Base.* [Wally McNamee/Corbis]

Andrews Air Force Base in Washington, D.C. Television cameras capture the transfer of the casket from the plane to an ambulance, and television announcers are silent as Jackie walks down the stairs.

Lyndon Johnson stands at news microphones to say his first public words as president: "This is a sad time for all people. We have suffered a loss that cannot be weighed. For me, it is a deep personal tragedy. I know that the world shares the sorrow that Mrs. Kennedy and her family bear. I will do my best. That is all I can do. I ask for your help—and God's."

The networks show the now heartbreaking footage of a smiling, vigorous Kennedy arriving at Love Field just that morning and plunging into the crowd to shake hands. Groups gather in front of

*Lee Harvey Oswald in police custody after his arrest. He was cut over his
eye during the scuffle at the movie theater.* [© Bettmann/Corbis/AP]

U.S. embassies in foreign countries. Former U.S. presidents and
leaders from around the world make statements.

And the world gets its first look at Lee Harvey Oswald as he is
led to his cell.

CHAPTER FORTY

NOVEMBER 23, 1963
White House

I N THE EAST ROOM OF THE WHITE HOUSE, John Kennedy's flag-draped casket lies on a curtained podium with honor guards always in attendance. Cameras capture members of the family as they walk into the building for a private mass. All day long, people pay their respects: former president Eisenhower, chief justice Earl Warren, the new president, family friends, senators, congressmen, and White House staff.

Robert Kennedy is assembling a list for the funeral on Monday. He sends a telegram to Martin Luther King Jr. inviting him to attend the funeral.

These two men cannot know that in five and a half years both will be dead at the hand of assassins.

The Honor Guard places President Kennedy's casket in the East Room of the White House. Mrs. Kennedy and Robert Kennedy are among the people near the door. [JFK Presidential Library and Museum]

*Members of the Honor Guard
remain with the casket at all times.*
[JFK Presidential Library and Museum]

Telegram . . . .
Day Letter . . . .
Night Message . .
Night Letter . . .

TELEGRAM
CORRESPONDENCE COPY

Party Sending

Time Filed
A. M.   P. M.

Date 847P EST NOV 23 63 AC254

To   DR MARTIN LUTHER KING

Place   RA484 R WA371 RX GOVT PD THE WHITE HOUSE
WASHINGTON DC 23 802 P EST

JA2-4596 ATLA 563 JOHNSON AVE

YOU ARE INVITED TO PARTICIPATE IN FUNERAL SERVICES FOR
PRESIDENT JOHN F. KENNEDY ON MONDAY, NOVEMBER 25 AT ST.
MATTHEW'S CATHEDRAL, WASHINGTON, D. C. WHEN YOU ARRIVE
IN WASHINGTON, PLEASE CONTACT THE CHIEF OF PROTOCOL,
DEPARTMENT OF STATE

ROBERT F KENNEDY

(02).

Above Message was sent prepaid.

*Robert Kennedy contacted leaders at home and heads of state
from around the world with details of his brother's funeral arrangements.*

CHAPTER FORTY-ONE

SUNDAY, NOVEMBER 24, 1963
Dallas Police Department

LEE HARVEY OSWALD ARRIVES at the Dallas Police Station at 2:00 P.M. on Friday. In the next 45 hours he will be interrogated for 12 hours, be placed in four lineups, receive visits from his wife, mother, and brother Robert, and sleep in a maximum-security cell.

At a press conference just after midnight on Sunday, Lee Harvey Oswald tells reporters that the police are after him because he has lived in the Soviet Union. He denies shooting the president and denies that he is part of a larger conspiracy.

The Dallas police do little to shield Oswald at that press conference. Reporters are allowed to physically crowd the handcuffed suspect.

Later on Sunday, Oswald is to be transferred to the county jail. He is led through the basement of the Dallas Police Department, apparently to a waiting armored car. Actually, the

Oswald gestures to the crowd surrounding him. [© Associated Press]

armored car is a decoy—for security reasons, the plan is to take Oswald to a police car instead.

A crowd of journalists watch the smiling Oswald as he makes his way down the corridor, his right arm handcuffed to the left arm of Detective J. R. Leavelle. Three television cameras roll.

"Here he comes!" someone shouts as Oswald emerges from the jail office.

One of those crowding around is Jack Ruby. He made his way into the police station with a Colt Cobra .38 in his coat pocket.

Jack Ruby is five foot nine inches tall and 175 pounds, and is fond of carrying a big roll of cash. He's a quick-tempered nightclub owner with friends in the Mafia and on the police force. Ruby considers himself a Democrat and a patriot. Like many Americans, he is infuriated by JFK's death and he wants revenge. He can't believe that Oswald is smiling. The crowd presses forward. Microphones

JACK RUBY'S REVOLVER

EVIDENCE

DATE
8•31•78

METROPOLITAN POLICE DEPT. WASH. D.C. 20001
CRIME SCENE EXAMINATION SECTION

are thrust at Oswald and questions shouted. Flashbulbs pop as photographers capture the moment for posterity. Oswald walks 10 feet outside the jail office, on his way to the ramp where the police car is waiting.

Suddenly, Jack Ruby emerges from the crowd. He moves fast, aiming his gun at Oswald's stomach, and fires one shot. The time is 11:21 A.M.

Jack Ruby is set upon by police. Lee Harvey Oswald slumps and is immediately transported to Parkland Hospital. After arriving, he

is placed in Trauma Room Two, right across the hall from the emergency room where John Kennedy spent the final minutes of his life. At 1:07 P.M., 48 hours and seven minutes after JFK's death, Lee Harvey Oswald also dies.

Left: *Jack Ruby shoots Lee Harvey Oswald in the stomach.* [Bob Jackson, AP/Dallas-Times Herald]

Below: *Jack Ruby talks to the press during his lawyer's effort to move his trial away from Dallas.* [© Bettmann/Corbis]

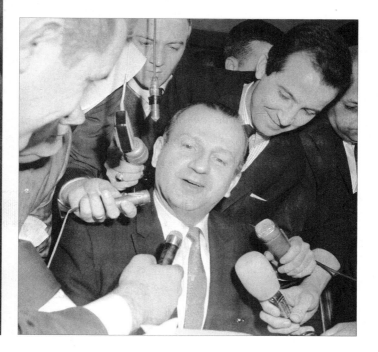

THE MAKING OF
A LEGEND

CHAPTER FORTY-TWO

NOVEMBER 24—25, 1963
Washington, D.C.

J OHN F. KENNEDY'S CASKET IS LOADED onto a caisson, a
two-wheeled military cart, drawn by seven white horses,
and carried down Pennsylvania Avenue to the U.S. Capitol to
lie in state. A single black horse follows the casket. It has no
rider, just a sword strapped to the saddle and boots placed back-
wards in the stirrups. All over the world, this riderless horse is a
symbol of a fallen soldier.

At the Capitol, John Jr. is led away by an aide. Jackie
Kennedy and her daughter, Caroline, stand beside the casket.
Jackie's dignity touches everyone who sees her.

After a brief ceremony, the family leaves and the public
begins filing past. They have waited in line, some for as long as
10 hours, to pay their respects to President John Fitzgerald

November 24, 1963: A horse-drawn caisson carrying John Kennedy's casket leaves
the White House en route to the Capitol Building, where the casket will lie in state.
[JFK Presidential Library and Museum]

November 25, 1963: Mrs. Kennedy and Caroline kneel at the president's casket in the Capitol Building. [© Bettmann/Corbis]

Robert Kennedy, Jackie Kennedy, and Edward Kennedy lead the funeral procession from the White House to St. Matthew's Cathedral. Among the people behind them are the president of France, the emperor of Ethiopia, the queen of Greece, the vice-chancellor of Germany, and the king of Belgium. [JFK Presidential Library and Museum]

Kennedy. Television will show the slow procession all through the night until 9:00 the next morning.

Heads of state from around the world begin arriving at the airports.

Monday, November 25

The funeral on Monday at St. Matthew's Cathedral is televised, watched by an estimated 180 million people around the world. Nineteen heads of state and three reigning monarchs attend. After the service, the casket is once again carried to the caisson. Jackie Kennedy and Caroline and John stand as it passes. Mrs. Kennedy reaches down and whispers to young John. The three-year-old then salutes as the casket passes by.

The final procession to Arlington National Cemetery is miles long. At the grave site, bagpipes play and 49 jet planes zoom overhead, one for each state with one missing, followed by *Air Force One*, which dips a wing over the grave in salute to the fallen president.

As a final gesture, Jackie Kennedy bends to light an eternal flame that will mark the grave site. The funeral is over.

———

For the next days, months, and years, people will discuss and debate the contributions, accomplishments, and failures of John Fitzgerald Kennedy's 1,036 days in office. His legacy will thrive in institutions such as the Peace Corps, in scientific efforts such as landing a man on the moon, in the Civil Rights Act of 1964. And he will be forever credited with stopping a nuclear war with the Soviet Union. But most of all, Kennedy will be remembered as an inspiration to a generation of young people, urging them to reach for ideals and use their talents wisely in service to their fellow men.

The funeral procession crosses the Lincoln Memorial Bridge to Arlington National Cemetery. Black Jack, the riderless horse, follows the caisson. [© Wally McNamee/Corbis]

CHAPTER FORTY-THREE

THE KENNEDY LEGACY

AFTER THE ASSASSINATION, people mythologized John Kennedy. The slain leader grew larger than life in people's memories. Decades after his assassination, we still see evidence of his influence and inspiration around us.

A Man on the Moon: The Space Program

On May 25, 1961, in an address to Congress, President Kennedy said, "I believe that this nation should commit itself to achieving the goal, before

The Rocket Garden at the Kennedy Space Center.
[© Edwin Verin/Shutterstock.com]

this decade is out, of landing a man on the moon and returning him safely to Earth." He went on to allocate millions of dollars to the space program. Kennedy's dream was fulfilled on July 20, 1969, when Neil Armstrong became the first human to set foot on the moon. Edwin "Buzz" Aldrin Jr. and Michael Collins were the other astronauts on that historic journey.

A few days after the assassination, President Johnson proposed that NASA's Cape Canaveral be renamed the John F. Kennedy Space Center. The Center remains central to the nation's space program.

A Showcase for the Arts:
The John F. Kennedy Center for the Performing Arts

The John F. Kennedy Center for the Performing Arts recognizes the role the president and his wife played in supporting the arts by offering artists a showcase in their televised concerts from the East Room, among many other efforts. Plans for a National Cultural Center began in 1958 when Dwight D. Eisenhower was president. During Kennedy's term, he raised funds for the project and named his wife, Jackie, and Mrs. Eisenhower as honorary co-chairs of the institution. Since the Kennedy Center's opening in 1971, it has been one of the most important cultural institutions in the country, presenting dance, ballet, chamber, jazz,

A sculpture of the head of the fallen president inside the John F. Kennedy Center for the Performing Arts in Washington, D.C. [LOC, DIG-highsm-12385]

*The John F. Kennedy Center is the busiest performing arts
facility in the United States.* [Maisna/Shutterstock.com]

folk, and multimedia concerts, theater, art exhibitions, and lectures
for people of all ages. Kennedy Center honorees are named each
year in a grand celebration that is shown on television a day or two
after Christmas.

The dramatic building stands next to the Potomac River near
the Lincoln Memorial.

A Ban on Nuclear Testing: Nuclear Test Ban Treaties

When John Kennedy took office, both the United States and Russia had enough nuclear weapons stockpiled to destroy the planet.
As more powerful bombs were invented, they were tested

by detonating them underground, in the ocean, or in space. Each explosion released radioactive particles into the atmosphere, which then fell to Earth as radioactive fallout. Radiation can permanently damage human cells and cause a wide range of illnesses, as well as contaminate the environment.

After the Cuban missile crisis brought the world very close to nuclear war, Kennedy and Premier Khrushchev began to talk about setting limits on testing. On August 5, 1963, the Limited Nuclear Test Ban Treaty was signed. It banned testing in space and underwater but allowed it underground. Kennedy struggled to get the Senate to approve the treaty. It was finally ratified and signed into law on October 7.

Efforts to pass a comprehensive nuclear test ban treaty that would prohibit testing in all environments, including underground, continue to this day. The United Nations General Assembly adopted a treaty in 1996, although not enough countries have signed it.

American Ambassadors to the World: The Peace Corps
On October 14, 1960, then Senator Kennedy gave a speech at the University of Michigan. He said:

> *How many of you who are going to be doctors are willing to spend your days in Ghana? Technicians or engineers, how many of you are willing to work in the Foreign Service and spend your lives traveling around the world? On your willingness to do that, not merely to serve one year or two years in the service, but*

President Kennedy greets 600 Peace Corps volunteers on the South Lawn of the White House, August 1962. [JFK Presidential Library and Museum]

on your willingness to contribute part of your life to this country, I think will depend the answer whether a free society can compete.

The Peace Corps traces its roots and its mission to this speech. It thrives today as a government agency devoted to world peace and friendship. Volunteers spend two years in developing countries providing education, environmental preservation, and communication infrastructure and responding to many other areas of need. Americans have served as Peace Corps volunteers in 139 countries since the program was founded.

An Elite Fighting Team:
U.S. Navy SEALs

In 1962, President Kennedy established the Navy SEALs to train for "unconventional warfare." These specialists conduct hazardous missions that large, highly visible units could not. It was a team of SEALs who found and killed Osama bin Laden.

Kennedy talks with U.S. Navy SEALs, April 1962.
[JFK Presidential Library and Museum]

A Distinctive Hat:
U.S. Army Green Berets

The Green Berets are U.S. Army Special Forces. They are also trained in unconventional warfare. Named after the soft green hats that Kennedy authorized, they specialize in foreign internal defense, hostage rescue, and counterterrorism.

EPILOGUE

AFTER JOHN F. KENNEDY WAS BURIED and Lyndon Johnson took over as president, I began hearing a lot about Vietnam. Some of what I heard came from TV reports about the war and the demonstrations against it. By senior year in high school, older boys I knew from the neighborhood began coming back from Vietnam. Some came home injured. Some came home with altered personalities. I talked to some of them, and they each said the same thing: Vietnam was chaos; there was nothing good about it. I was about to graduate and maybe get drafted. Their stories scared me.

I went to college and so was deferred from the draft. It seemed like a good thing to do, and I studied and played sports, determined to stay in school. There was time for a few extra activities, so I started writing for the college newspaper, *The Circle*. That made me pay attention to politics more closely. But my heroes continued to be men who played sports: Willie Mays, the legendary Giants center fielder, and Jim Brown of the Cleveland Browns.

In 1969, my junior year in college, I joined a year-abroad program and went to London, England. Every day of that trip opened my eyes more. I was no longer just a suburban boy. I saw places I had only read about in textbooks. As a history major, that trip was like a candy store.

But one part of that year in Europe really made me who I am today. At the time, people all over the world were upset and angry with Americans, some because of Vietnam and others simply because they did not like our political system or the way we act: big, bold, and vocal. Kids made fun of my accent (New York), of American television shows (*American*

Bandstand), and of my preoccupation with following that strange American game (football).

To this day, I can recall the feelings I had that year when people made fun of the U.S.A. All that anti-Americanism made me think a lot about pride and loyalty. I realized that I love my country fiercely even though it's not perfect, and believe strongly in our system of government.

After college, I had to find a way to use my history major in a way that I hoped might help people. Warm, sunny Miami, Florida, was the location of a high school teaching job. It was tough, but I lasted two years, and think I did an okay job presenting kids with both sides of lots of issues in history. Then I started on the journey that has led to my television success today. Like most career paths, mine started small in places like Scranton, Pennsylvania; Denver, Colorado; and Dallas, Texas.

The author heads to England and beyond.

In 1977, I was an investigative reporter for WFAA-TV in Dallas. The Kennedy assassination was in the news again. The House of Representatives was investigating both the Kennedy and Martin Luther King Jr. assassinations

George de Mohrenschildt in 1964.
[© Bettmann/Corbis]

again to see if there was evidence of conspiracy in either tragedy. When I looked at the story, I saw some loose ends. One was George de Mohrenschildt, the Russian-American businessman who had befriended the Oswalds.

I tracked him down at his daughter's home in Florida. By some awful coincidence, the day I went to see him there, he had also gotten a request to be interviewed by the House Committee on Assassinations. As I knocked on the door, I heard a shotgun blast. He had killed himself. Later, the chairman of the House committee said de Mohrenschildt was a "crucial witness." I often wonder what I might have been able to find out. To this day, his relationship to Lee Harvey Oswald is not fully understood.

Over the years, my list of personal heroes has developed. I have looked at our country's history and paid close attention to people who tried to protect the United States and change it for the good and to people who took on huge world problems alone or with little help: Abraham Lincoln, who ended the Civil War and forced the country to stay united; Franklin Roosevelt, who led the country through the Great Depression and World War II; Mother Teresa, who devoted her life to tackling the dire poverty in the slums of Calcutta, India; Bono, who champions the civil rights and social causes of Africans; and Bobby Kennedy, who used the power of his office as U.S. attorney general to further the cause of civil rights.

In 1966, Bobby Kennedy said,

> *Few will have the greatness to bend history itself; but each of us can work to change a small portion of the events, and in the total of all those acts will be written the history of this generation. . . . It is from numberless diverse acts of courage and belief that human history is thus shaped. Each time a man stands up for an ideal, or acts to improve the lot of others, or strikes out against injustice, he sends forth a tiny ripple of hope, and crossing each other from a million different centers of energy and daring, those ripples build a current that can sweep down the mightiest walls of oppression and resistance.*

The author as a first-year teacher in Miami.

He was echoing the meaning of one of John Fitzgerald Kennedy's favorite quotes. It's from a poem by Dante, who lived in Italy in the Middle Ages: "The hottest places in Hell are reserved for those who in time of moral crisis preserve their neutrality."

Today, I take those words to heart. If I see injustice, I say something. As you think about John Fitzgerald Kennedy, I hope that you will appreciate the ways in which he tried to bend history. He was president for only 1,036 days. Who knows what he might have accomplished if he had lived? His death filled the country with sorrow because he represented a grand American vision of pride, fairness, and service to one's country.

AFTERWORD

JOHN KENNEDY'S BURIAL SITE at Arlington Cemetery is lit by an eternal flame, suggested by Jackie Kennedy. It burns at the center of a five-foot circular slab of Cape Cod granite. Jackie rests next to him, as do their two deceased infants, Arabella and Patrick. Television coverage of John Kennedy's funeral transformed Arlington from the burial place of soldiers and sailors into a popular tourist destination. To this day, no place in Arlington has more visitors than the grave of John Fitzgerald Kennedy. Generations after his assassination, more than four million people a year arrive to pay their respects to the fallen president.

Jackie Kennedy's enormous grief, and the grace with which she handled herself after the assassination, only enhanced the public admiration she earned during her husband's presidency. In 1968, she married Aristotle Onassis, a Greek businessman. Sadly, the 69-year-old Onassis died of respiratory failure just seven years after their marriage, making Jackie a widow for the second time at the young age of 46. After Onassis's death, Jackie retreated from the public eye, eventually becoming a book editor in New York City and editing the books of people as diverse as singers Michael Jackson and Carly Simon, and Egyptian novelist Naguib Mahfouz, a Nobel laureate. She died on May 19, 1994, from non-Hodgkin's lymphoma at the age of 64. She is buried at Arlington National Cemetery next to John Kennedy.

Caroline Kennedy grew up to attend Radcliffe College and later earn her law degree from Columbia University. She married author and designer

The Kennedy grave site in Arlington National Cemetery. [LOC, DIG-highsm-18141]

Edwin Schlossberg, whom she met while she was working at the Metropolitan Museum of Art in New York City. They have three children. Ms. Kennedy is an author and speaker and volunteers her time to charitable organizations.

John F. Kennedy Jr. became a symbol for the tragic history of the Kennedy family. The image of him on his third birthday saluting his father's coffin broke hearts worldwide. Erroneously thought to be nicknamed "John-John"—that name was fabricated by the press—John Jr. attended college at Brown University and then went on to the New York University School of Law and worked in the Manhattan district attorney's office. On July 16, 1999, he was piloting a small plane when it crashed into the Atlantic Ocean off the coast of Martha's Vineyard. The accident killed John Kennedy Jr.; his wife, Carolyn Bessette-Kennedy; and her sister, Lauren. He was 38 years old. His ashes, and those of his wife, were scattered at sea.

President Johnson signs the Civil Rights Act into law on July 2, 1964. Martin Luther King Jr. and others witness this historic moment. [LBJ Library]

Lyndon Baines Johnson inherited a great deal of unfinished business from the Kennedy administration. He masterfully cobbled together coalitions within Congress to help pass the historic Civil Rights Act of 1964. Johnson, working closely with Martin Luther King Jr., framed the issue in terms of JFK's legacy in order to gather support for the act. However, Vietnam was an inherited headache that proved to be his undoing. As the antiwar movement gained traction, LBJ, fearing defeat, chose not to run again in 1968. Upon leaving Washington, he returned to his Texas ranch, where he died of a heart attack at the age of 64 on January 22, 1973.

Bobby Kennedy was devastated by his brother's assassination. He continued in his role as U.S. attorney general for nine months and then decided to run for the U.S. Senate. He was elected and served for four years. Then, in 1968, he launched a bid for the presidency. On the night he won a major victory in the California primary, he gave a brief speech at the Ambassador Hotel. Just past midnight on June 5, 1968, Bobby Kennedy was assassinated by a disturbed lone gunman, Sirhan Sirhan. Kennedy lived for 26 hours before dying on June 6, 1968, at the age of 42.

Robert F. Kennedy, September 25, 1963.
[LOC, DIG-ds-00976]

Jack Ruby, whose real name was Jacob Rubinstein, argued that he shot Lee Harvey Oswald to redeem the city of Dallas for the assassination. At trial, he was convicted of murder with malice and sentenced to death. He was eventually awarded a new trial after a judge agreed that Ruby could not have received a fair trial in Dallas, due to the enormous publicity surrounding the shooting. But before the new trial could get under way, Ruby was admitted to Parkland Hospital for symptoms of the flu. Instead, he was found to have cancer in his liver, lungs, and brain. He died of a pulmonary embolism on January 3, 1967, at the age of 55. Jack Ruby is buried next to his parents in Westlawn Cemetery, in Norridge, Illinois.

Martin Luther King Jr. continued his civil rights crusade and became one of the world's most admired men. He was named *Time* magazine's Man of the Year in 1963. On December 10 of that year, he was awarded the Nobel Peace Prize. On April 4, 1968, King was shot down in Memphis, Tennessee, by an assassin named James Earl Ray, a racist who escaped to Canada, and then to England, before being arrested for the murder of Dr. King. On November 2, 1986, a national holiday was declared in King's honor.

The Oswald family history is complicated and not always clear. Lee Harvey's father, Robert E. Lee Oswald, died before Lee was born. He served in World War I and is buried in New Orleans. He was Lee's mother's second husband.

Lee did not have a father figure in his life. He and his mother moved 21 times before he joined the Marines at age 17. In her testimony before the Warren Commission, Marguerite Oswald said her son read a lot and liked to keep score watching football games on TV. She does not mention that school officials thought he might have a personality disorder.

Marguerite Oswald spent the years after the assassination attempting to convince people that Lee Harvey Oswald was innocent. She lectured to

A time capsule honoring Martin Luther King Jr. was buried under
Freedom Plaza at 14th Street and Pennsylvania Avenue in Washington, D.C.
It will be opened in 2088. [LOC, highsm-14536]

groups and even made a recording reading the letters Lee sent to her from Russia. She died in 1981 at the age of 73.

Marina Prusakova Oswald was whisked away to a hotel right after Oswald was shot. There, the FBI interviewed her for hours. A few months later, she testified before the Warren Commission. Marina remarried in 1965 and

Marina Oswald holding June, Robert Oswald, and Marguerite Oswald holding Rachel, at Lee Harvey Oswald's funeral. [© Corbis]

became a U.S. citizen in 1989. She has appeared in several documentaries about Lee Harvey Oswald and the assassination.

Lee Harvey Oswald's daughters, **June and Rachel**, were very young in 1963. Their mother protected them from the press and waited about six years to tell them about their father. Both girls took their stepfather's name.

Robert Oswald, born in 1934, is five years older than Lee Harvey Oswald. He was in military high schools and then in the Marines while Lee was growing up.

Robert remembers that Lee had a vivid imagination and thought he could be anybody and do anything he wanted. In a 1993 interview, Robert said, "I think I've come to an understanding of Lee. . . . I watched the deterioration of a human being. You look at the last year—his work, his family, trying to go to Cuba. . . . Everything is deteriorating. It was a terrible thing to look at."

Robert paid $710 for Lee Harvey Oswald's funeral, which took place on the same day as President John F. Kennedy's and Officer J. D. Tippit's.

THE KENNEDYS: A PHOTO FAMILY TREE

The Kennedy family on the lawn of their Boston home on July 8, 1934. [© Bettmann/Corbis]

JEAN ANN KENNEDY
b. 1928

PATRICIA KENNEDY
1924–2006

KATHLEEN
AGNES KENNE
1920–1948

EDWARD MOORE
KENNEDY
1932–2009

ROBERT FRANCIS
KENNEDY
1925–1968

EUNICE MARY
KENNEDY
1921–2009

not shown: JOSEPH PATRICK KENNEDY JR.
1915–1944

ROSEMARY KENNEDY
1918–2005

ROSE ELIZABETH KENNEDY
1890–1995

JOHN FITZGERALD
KENNEDY
1917–1963

JOSEPH PATRICK
KENNEDY SR.
1888–1969

You can read biographies of each of John Kennedy's eight siblings and their parents on
the John F. Kennedy Presidential Library and Museum website (www.jfklibrary.org).

Some of the crew of PT-109.   [JFK Presidential Library and Museum]

THE CREW OF USS *PT-109* ON ITS LAST MISSION

(In order by rank)

Lieutenant (junior grade) John F. Kennedy	*Commanding Officer* (standing, far right)
Ensign Leonard Jay Thom	*Executive Officer* (bottom row, far right)
Ensign George Henry Robertson Ross	*Lookout / Gunner*
QM3C Edman Edgar Mauer	*Quartermaster, cook, and signalman* (top row, 3rd from left)
RM2C John E. Maguire	*Radioman* (top row, 2nd from right)
S1C Raymond Albert	*Gunner*
GM3C Charles A. Harris	*Gunner* (bottom row, far left)
MOMM1C Gerard E. Zinser	*Motor mechanic*
MOMM1C Patrick Henry McMahon	*Motor mechanic*
MOMM2C Harold W. Marney*	*Gunner*
MOMM2C William Johnston	*Gunner*
TM2C Raymond L. Starkey	*Torpedoman*
TM2C Andrew Jackson Kirksey*	*Torpedoman* (bottom row, 2nd from right)

Killed in action

JOHN F. KENNEDY'S
INAUGURAL ADDRESS

Delivered on January 20, 1961

- - -

Vice President Johnson, Mr. Speaker, Mr. Chief
Justice, President Eisenhower, Vice President
Nixon, President Truman, reverend clergy, fellow
citizens:

We observe today not a victory of party, but a
celebration of freedom—symbolizing an end as well
as a beginning—signifying renewal as well as
change. For I have sworn before you and Almighty
God the same solemn oath our forebears prescribed
nearly a century and three-quarters ago.

The world is very different now. For man holds in
his mortal hands the power to abolish all forms
of human poverty and all forms of human life. And
yet the same revolutionary beliefs for which our
forebears fought are still at issue around the
globe—the belief that the rights of man come not
from the generosity of the state, but from the
hand of God.

We dare not forget today that we are the heirs of
that first revolution. Let the word go forth from
this time and place, to friend and foe alike,

*Kennedy's inaugural remarks were addressed not only
to the American people but also to citizens in friendly
countries and those in less friendly ones.* [© Bettmann/Corbis]

that the torch has been passed to a new generation
of Americans—born in this century, tempered by war,
disciplined by a hard and bitter peace, proud of our
ancient heritage, and unwilling to witness or permit
the slow undoing of those human rights to which this
nation has always been committed, and to which we are
committed today at home and around the world.

Let every nation know, whether it wishes us well or
ill, that we shall pay any price, bear any burden,
meet any hardship, support any friend, oppose any foe
to assure the survival and the success of liberty.

This much we pledge—and more.

To those old allies whose cultural and spiritual
origins we share, we pledge the loyalty of faithful
friends. United there is little we cannot do in a host
of cooperative ventures. Divided there is little we
can do—for we dare not meet a powerful challenge at
odds and split asunder.

To those new states whom we welcome to the ranks of
the free, we pledge our word that one form of colonial
control shall not have passed away merely to be re-
placed by a far more iron tyranny. We shall not always
expect to find them supporting our view. But we shall
always hope to find them strongly supporting their own
freedom—and to remember that, in the past, those who
foolishly sought power by riding the back of the tiger
ended up inside.

To those people in the huts and villages of half the
globe struggling to break the bonds of mass misery, we
pledge our best efforts to help them help themselves,
for whatever period is required—not because the Communists may be doing it, not because we seek their

votes, but because it is right. If a free society cannot help the many who are poor, it cannot save the few who are rich.

To our sister republics south of our border, we offer a special pledge: to convert our good words into good deeds, in a new alliance for progress, to assist free men and free governments in casting off the chains of poverty. But this peaceful revolution of hope cannot become the prey of hostile powers. Let all our neighbors know that we shall join with them to oppose aggression or subversion anywhere in the Americas. And let every other power know that this hemisphere intends to remain the master of its own house.

To that world assembly of sovereign states, the United Nations, our last best hope in an age where the instruments of war have far outpaced the instruments of peace, we renew our pledge of support—to prevent it from becoming merely a forum for invective, to strengthen its shield of the new and the weak, and to enlarge the area in which its writ may run.

Finally, to those nations who would make themselves our adversary, we offer not a pledge but a request: that both sides begin anew the quest for peace, before the dark powers of destruction unleashed by science engulf all humanity in planned or accidental self-destruction.

We dare not tempt them with weakness. For only when our arms are sufficient beyond doubt can we be certain beyond doubt that they will never be employed.

But neither can two great and powerful groups of nations take comfort from our present course—both sides overburdened by the cost of modern weapons, both

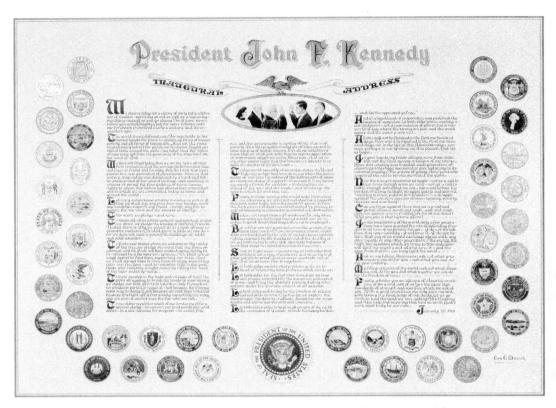

A gift to President Kennedy from E. E. Mizerek. The text of his inaugural address is bordered by the seals of the 50 states. [JFK Presidential Library and Museum]

rightly alarmed by the steady spread of the deadly atom, yet both racing to alter that uncertain balance of terror that stays the hand of mankind's final war.

So let us begin anew—remembering on both sides that civility is not a sign of weakness, and sincerity is always subject to proof. Let us never negotiate out of fear. But let us never fear to negotiate.

Let both sides explore what problems unite us instead of belaboring those problems which divide us.

Let both sides, for the first time, formulate serious and precise proposals for the inspection and control of arms, and bring the absolute power to destroy other nations under the absolute control of all nations.

Let both sides seek to invoke the wonders of science instead of its terrors. Together let us explore the stars, conquer the deserts, eradicate disease, tap the ocean depths, and encourage the arts and commerce.

Let both sides unite to heed, in all corners of the earth, the command of Isaiah—to "undo the heavy burdens, and [to] let the oppressed go free."

And, if a beachhead of cooperation may push back the jungle of suspicion, let both sides join in creating a new endeavor—not a new balance of power, but a new world of law—where the strong are just, and the weak secure, and the peace preserved.

All this will not be finished in the first one hundred days. Nor will it be finished in the first one thousand days; nor in the life of this Administration; nor even perhaps in our lifetime on this planet. But let us begin.

In your hands, my fellow citizens, more than mine, will rest the final success or failure of our course. Since this country was founded, each generation of Americans has been summoned to give testimony to its national loyalty. The graves of young Americans who answered the call to service surround the globe.

Now the trumpet summons us again—not as a call to bear arms, though arms we need—not as a call to battle, though embattled we are—but a call to bear the burden of a long twilight struggle, year in and year out, "rejoicing in hope, patient in tribulation," a struggle against the common enemies of man: tyranny, poverty, disease, and war itself.

Can we forge against these enemies a grand and global alliance, North and South, East and West, that can assure a more fruitful life for all mankind? Will you join in that historic effort?

In the long history of the world, only a few generations have been granted the role of defending freedom in its hour of maximum danger. I do not shrink from this responsibility—I welcome it. I do not believe that any of us would exchange places with any other people or any other generation. The energy, the faith, the devotion which we bring to this endeavor will light our country and all who serve it. And the glow from that fire can truly light the world.

And so, my fellow Americans, ask not what your country can do for you—ask what you can do for your country.

My fellow citizens of the world, ask not what America will do for you, but what together we can do for the freedom of man.

Finally, whether you are citizens of America or citizens of the world, ask of us here the same high standards of strength and sacrifice which we ask of you. With a good conscience our only sure reward, with history the final judge of our deeds, let us go forth to lead the land we love, asking His blessing and His help, but knowing that here on earth God's work must truly be our own.

JOHN AND JACKIE KENNEDY: SOME FAMOUS AND INTERESTING WORDS

John Kennedy

◇ My fellow Americans, ask not what your country can do for you—ask what you can do for your country.

◇ Let the word go forth from this time and place, to friend and foe alike, that the torch has been passed to a new generation of Americans—born in this century, tempered by war, disciplined by a hard and bitter peace. . . .

◇ Change is the law of life. And those who look only to the past or the present are certain to miss the future.

◇ Let every nation know, whether it wishes us well or ill, that we shall pay any price, bear any burden, meet any hardship, support any friend, oppose any foe to assure the survival and the success of liberty.

◇ If we cannot end now our differences, at least we can help make the world safe for diversity.

◇ The best road to progress is freedom's road.

◇ Conformity is the jailer of freedom and the enemy of growth.

◇ Physical fitness is not only one of the most important keys to a healthy body, it is the basis of dynamic and creative intellectual activity.

◇ The time to repair the roof is when the sun is shining.

◇ In a very real sense, it will not be one man going to the moon; it will be an entire nation. For all of us must work to put him there.

◇ Mankind must put an end to war, or war will put an end to mankind.

◇ I am the man who accompanied Jacqueline Kennedy to Paris, and I have enjoyed it.

Jackie Kennedy

◇ If you bungle raising your children, I don't think whatever else you do well matters very much.

◇ A camel makes an elephant feel like a jet plane.

◇ There are many little ways to enlarge your child's world. Love of books is the best of all.

◇ Now I think that I should have known that he was magic all along. I did know it—but I should have guessed that it would be too much to ask to grow old with and see our children grow up together. So now, he is a legend when he would have preferred to be a man.

President De Gaulle welcomes Jackie Kennedy to Paris on May 31, 1961. [© Bettmann/Corbis]

This portrait was taken in September 1961, when the Kennedys were visiting friends in Newport, Rhode Island. [JFK Presidential Library and Museum]

THE ZAPRUDER FILM:
A MOMENT-BY-MOMENT RECORD

O**N FRIDAY, NOVEMBER 22, 1963,** Abraham Zapruder, an executive of a Dallas clothing company, spent his lunch hour in Dealey Plaza. He used an 8mm camera to film the passing motorcade carrying John Kennedy, his wife, and other dignitaries. His camera caught the moments when the president was shot. Zapruder returned to his office and asked his assistant to call the police or find a Secret Service man. Agent Forrest Sorrels in the Dallas Secret Service office took the film to the local Eastman Kodak processing plant to be developed. The film captured 26.6 seconds in 486 frames of film.

Zapruder's color film was used by the Warren Commission and is crucial to all experts who try to re-create the events of that day. Zapruder was shaken by what he saw through the lens. He wept when interviewed about the assassination even years later.

You can watch the film on YouTube.

Abraham Zapruder was standing at the west end of the colonnade, taking movie film when Kennedy was shot. [William A. Mueller/Shutterstock.com]

INVESTIGATING THE ASSASSINATION: THE WARREN COMMISSION

ON NOVEMBER 29, 1963, one week after President Kennedy was assassinated, President Johnson announced the formation of a commission to investigate the event. The group, which was formally named the President's Commission on the Assassination of President Kennedy, was led by the chief justice of the Supreme Court, Earl Warren. Its seven other members included Gerald R. Ford, then a representative from Michigan, who would become the 38th president after Richard Nixon resigned, and Allen W. Dulles, former director of the CIA under President Kennedy.

With thoroughness and speed, the Warren Commission, as it came to be called, interviewed 552 witnesses and considered 3,100 exhibits. It took testimony from 10 federal intelligence agencies, including the Secret Service, the FBI, the CIA, military intelligence, and the Department of State.

The final report, submitted just 10 months later on September 24, 1964, was 888 pages long. A few months later, the commission published 26 volumes of evidence that it had reviewed and more

JFK chats with Supreme Court chief justice Earl Warren and his wife, Nina, before a dinner at the White House.
[JFK Presidential Library and Museum]

Chief Justice Warren hands President Johnson the commission report.
The seven other members of the committee attend. Future president
Gerald Ford is fourth from the left. [LBJ Library]

than 50,000 pages of documents, memorandums, and transcripts of its meetings.

Lee Harvey Oswald never had a chance to defend himself in court, and so the commission did not have his testimony to consider. They took seriously their charge to be neutral fact finders and concluded that Oswald, alone and unaided, shot and killed President Kennedy and wounded Texas governor John Connally, and that Jack Ruby also acted alone. It found that the motivation for Oswald's act was his "urge to try to find a place in history" and that it was the product of his whole life, one "characterized by isolation, frustration, and failure."

The report also recommended changing the protocols for presidential security.

You can read the report at the National Archives website: www.archives.gov /research/jfk/warren-commission-report.

SOME FACTS
ABOUT THE EARLY 1960s

THE EARLY 1960S LOOKED BACK to the fifties a little bit in style and fashion but began to change when the Kennedys moved in to the White House in 1961. Glamour was in vogue. Young people began to loosen up, dancing the twist and watching *West Side Story*. Here are some top lists from the year 1961 (unless otherwise noted).

AT THE DANCE

"The Twist"
song by Chubby Checker

"The Locomotion"
song by Little Eva

"The Pony"
song by Chubby Checker

"The Watusi"
song by the Orlons

"It's Mashed Potato Time" song by Dee Dee Sharp

DOING YOUR HAIR

Beehive
Flip
French Roll
Bob
Pageboy

Important
tool:
a bristle brush
to tease
your hair

ON THE ROAD

Economy Domestic Compact Cars
Rambler   Falcon
Lark   Corvair
Valiant

Top-of-the-Line Luxury Cars
Ambassador   Buick Special
Thunderbird   Oldsmobile F-85

Top Imported Cars
VW Beetle • Opel • Fiat • Triumph
Renault Dauphine

ON TV

Wagon Train
Bonanza
Gunsmoke
Perry Mason
The Red Skelton Show
Candid Camera
Alfred Hitchcock Presents
The Twilight Zone
Mister Ed
Dr. Kildare

AT THE MOVIES

The Guns of Navarone   The Misfits
The Parent Trap   The Hustler
101 Dalmatians   West Side Story
Breakfast at Tiffany's   Babes in Toyland
Judgment at Nuremberg

"Will You Love Me Tomorrow"
by the Shirelles

"Wonderland by Night"
by Bert Kaempfert

"Calcutta"
by Lawrence Welk

"Pony Time"
by Chubby Checker

"Surrender"
by Elvis Presley

"Blue Moon"
by the Marcels

"Runaway"
by Del Shannon

NEW FOODS AT THE TABLE 1961–1963

Boiling bags of vegetables, some with butter sauce
Life cereal
Total cereal
Mrs. Butterworth's syrup
Coffee-Mate nondairy creamer
Dry roasted peanuts
Maxwell House freeze-dried instant coffee
Fruit Loops cereal
ChipsAhoy! Cookies
Tab diet soda

BESTSELLING CHILDREN'S BOOKS

The Phantom Tollbooth
by Norton Juster

James and the Giant Peach
by Roald Dahl

Once a Mouse . . .
by Marcia Brown

The Sneetches, and Other Stories
by Dr. Seuss

The Bronze Bow
by Elizabeth George Speare

Go, Dog, Go!
by P. D. Eastman

Where the Red Fern Grows
by Wilson Rawls

BESTSELLING ADULT BOOKS

Catch-22 by Joseph Heller

Stranger in a Strange Land
by Robert Heinlein

Franny and Zooey
by J. D. Salinger

To Kill a Mockingbird
by Harper Lee

The Foundation Trilogy
by C. S. Lewis

Winter of Our Discontent
by John Steinbeck

Mastering the Art of French Cooking by Julia Child

Mila 18 by Leon Uris

The Spy Who Loved Me (James Bond #10) by Ian Fleming

The Making of the President, 1960 by Theodore White

ON THE FIELD AND ICE: SPORTS CONTESTS OF 1961

PLAY BALL! PLAY BALL! PLAY BALL! PLAY BALL!

NBA: Boston Celtics vs. St. Louis Hawks series: 4–1

NCAA Football: Alabama and Ohio set state records: 11-0-0 and 8-0-1

Ernie Davis of Syracuse won the Heisman Trophy

Stanley Cup: Chicago Blackhawks vs. Detroit Red Wings series: 4–2

World Series: New York Yankees vs. Cincinnati Reds series: 4–1

WHAT THINGS COST

First-class stamp	$0.04
One gallon of gas	$0.27
One dozen eggs	$0.30
Movie ticket	$0.50
Fast-food hamburger	$0.20
Loaf of bread	$0.21
One-year subscription to *Motor Trend* magazine	$0.35

Average annual household income $5,315

Candy bar $0.05
Pack of gum $0.05

CINEMA TICKET
★ ★ ★
ADMIT ONE
31769

TIME LINE

May 29, 1917	John Fitzgerald Kennedy is born to Joseph and Rose Kennedy on Beals Street in Brookline, Massachusetts.
August 26, 1920	The Nineteenth Amendment is adopted. It gives women the right to vote.
September 12, 1924	John begins kindergarten at Edward Devotion School.
May 20, 1927	Captain Charles Lindbergh leaves New York in the plane the *Spirit of St. Louis* for the first solo nonstop flight across the Atlantic Ocean.
September 1927	The Kennedy family moves from Massachusetts to New York.
October 29, 1929	U.S. stock prices drop precipitously, causing the Great Depression.
September 19, 1931	John begins his freshman year at the Choate School, a private high school in Wallingford, Connecticut.
March 4, 1933	Franklin Delano Roosevelt is sworn in as the 32nd president of the United States.
December 1935	John has a serious case of hepatitis and is forced to withdraw from college.

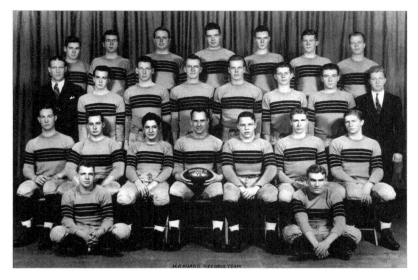

The 1937 Harvard junior varsity football team. Kennedy is standing third from the right in the third row. [JFK Presidential Library and Museum]

January 7, 1938 FDR appoints Joseph Kennedy to be ambassador to Great Britain.

June 20, 1940 John graduates *cum laude* from Harvard.

October 8, 1941 John joins the U.S. Navy Reserves.

December 7, 1941 Japan attacks Pearl Harbor.

December 8, 1941 The U.S. declares war on Japan.

August 2, 1943 *PT-109* is sunk by a Japanese destroyer.

May 31, 1944 John enters a hospital in Massachusetts because of back problems.

June 12, 1944	John is awarded the Navy and Marine Corps Medal for heroic conduct as the commanding officer of *PT-109.*
August 12, 1944	John's older brother, Joe Jr., is killed on a mission over the English Channel.
April–June 1945	John covers the conference that drafts plans for the United Nations, as a reporter for the International News Service.
August 6, 1945	The U.S. drops the first atomic bomb on Hiroshima, Japan. More than 140,000 people are killed instantly. As many as 30,000 more die of radiation poisoning within months.
August 14, 1945	Japan surrenders.
April 25, 1946	John announces his candidacy for the Democratic congressional seat from the Massachusetts Eleventh Congressional District.
June 18, 1946	John wins his party's nomination.
November 5, 1946	John is elected to the House of Representatives.
November 2, 1948	John is elected for a second term.
June 25, 1950	North Korea invades the Republic of Korea.
November 7, 1950	John is elected for a third term.
April 7, 1952	John announces his candidacy for the U.S. Senate.

November 4, 1952 John is elected to the Senate. Eisenhower is elected to the presidency with Richard Nixon as his vice president.

September 12, 1953 John Fitzgerald Kennedy marries 24-year-old Jacqueline Lee Bouvier.

May 17, 1954 The Supreme Court rules in *Brown v. Board of Education* that racial segregation in public schools is illegal.

October 21, 1954 John has back surgery. He writes *Profiles in Courage* during his recovery.

February 1955 John has follow-up back surgery.

May 6, 1957 *Profiles in Courage* wins the Pulitzer Prize in the biography category.

October 4, 1957 Russia launches an artificial space satellite, *Sputnik I.*

November 27, 1957 Caroline Kennedy is born.

November 4, 1958 John is reelected to the Senate.

January 1, 1959 Fidel Castro becomes leader of Cuba in a coup.

January 2, 1960 John announces his candidacy for president.

September 26, 1960 Kennedy and Richard Nixon, the Republican candidate, have their first of four televised debates.

November 8, 1960	Kennedy is elected 35th president of the United States.
November 25, 1960	John Fitzgerald Kennedy Jr. is born.
January 20, 1961	Kennedy is inaugurated. He is 43 years old.
March 1, 1961	Kennedy signs a bill establishing the Peace Corps.
March 29, 1961	Kennedy reorganizes the Council on Youth Fitness.
April 17, 1961	Bay of Pigs invasion fails.
May 5, 1961	The United States sends its first astronaut, Alan Shepard, into space.
May 11, 1961	The United States sends 400 Special Forces and 100 advisers to Vietnam.
May 14–20, 1961	Freedom riders are attacked in Birmingham, Anniston, and Montgomery, Alabama.
August 13, 1961	The Berlin Wall closes the border between East and West Berlin.
March 26, 1962	Kennedy gives Robert Frost the Congressional Medal of Honor.
September 30, 1962	Kennedy sends federal marshals to protect James Meredith, the first black student at the University of Mississippi.
October 16–28, 1962	The Cuban missile crisis unfolds.

Robert Frost, standing behind the microphones, was one of Kennedy's favorite poets. He often quoted from the poem "Stopping by Woods on a Snowy Evening." [JFK Presidential Library and Museum]

June 19, 1963   Kennedy sends a civil rights bill to Congress.

June 26, 1963   Kennedy visits West Berlin and delivers a speech at the Berlin Wall.

July 25, 1963   The Soviet Union, England, and the United States agree on a Limited Nuclear Test Ban treaty.

August 28, 1963   Martin Luther King Jr. delivers his famous "I Have a Dream" speech at the March on Washington.

October 26, 1963	Kennedy delivers a speech in tribute to Robert Frost, whose poem "Stopping by Woods on a Snowy Evening" is one Kennedy often quotes.
November 22, 1963	President John Fitzgerald Kennedy is assassinated in Dallas, Texas. He is 46 years old.
November 25, 1963	John Kennedy is buried in Arlington National Cemetery.

An eternal flame burns at the grave site of John and Jackie Kennedy. [© Larry Downing/Reuters/Corbis]

PLACES TO VISIT

THERE ARE HUNDREDS, PERHAPS THOUSANDS, of places around the world named for President John F. Kennedy. There are plazas, bridges, squares, and highways. There are schools and office buildings. His face has been on coins and stamps. Here is a selection of places that you can visit.

John F. Kennedy Space Center
www.nasa.gov/centers/kennedy/home/

NASA's Launch Operations Center at Cape Canaveral, Florida, was renamed the John F. Kennedy Space Center. You can tour the center in person, go to an astronaut training camp, and watch NASA launches online at their website.

The John F. Kennedy Presidential Library and Museum
www.JFKlibrary.org

The JFK Library on Columbia Point in Dorchester, Massachusetts, opened in 1979 as Kennedy's official presidential library. It has exhibits about the life of President Kennedy; his wife, Jackie; and his brother Robert, as well as displays about Kennedy's campaigns and his interest in the space program. You can visit in person or take a virtual tour of the museum online at their website. The website is the best source of information about John Kennedy, his life, and his political career.

The John F. Kennedy Center for the Performing Arts, Washington, D.C.
www.Kennedy-center.org

This grand building opened in 1971 in Washington, D.C., on the

*The John F. Kennedy Center for the Performing Arts
in Washington, D.C.* [Douglas Litchfield/Shutterstock.com]

Potomac River near the Lincoln Memorial. Its many stages showcase the performing arts: ballet, theater, orchestra, and opera. Free tours are offered every day.

*The Sixth Floor Museum at Dealey Plaza,
Dallas, Texas.* [Natalia Bratslavsky/Shutterstock.com]

The Sixth Floor Museum at Dealey Plaza, Dallas, Texas
Jfk.org

Maintained by the Dallas County Historical Foundation, the sixth floor of the building that was the Texas School Book Depository now houses a permanent exhibit on the assassination and legacy of John Kennedy.

John F. Kennedy Memorial Plaza in Dallas, Texas
Jfk.org

This square is not far from the site of President Kennedy's assassination. The memorial consists of an empty platform with "John Fitzgerald Kennedy" engraved along its side, surrounded by a concrete square enclosure with two openings. The architect said it symbolizes an open tomb, a tribute to JFK's living legacy.

John F. Kennedy Memorial Plaza in Dallas, Texas. [Carolyn DeVar/Shutterstock.com]

The John Fitzgerald Kennedy National Historic Site
Nps.gov/jofi

This National Parks site includes Kennedy's birthplace and childhood home at 83 Beals Street in Brookline, Massachusetts. From April through November you can tour his home and the neighborhood he grew up in. The president's mother, Rose Kennedy, restored the house to the way it was in 1917 when John Kennedy was born.

The White House
www.whitehouse.gov

Tours of the White House are available. You must ask your member of Congress for a ticket. To find your member of Congress, go to the website www.house.gov/representatives/find and type in your zip code. You may ask for a ticket up to six months in advance but not closer than twenty-one days before you want to visit. An interactive tour of the White House is available at www.whitehouse.gov/about/inside-white-house/interactive-tour.

THE AUTHOR RECOMMENDS . . .

RECOMMENDED READING

Byrne, Paul J. *The Cuban Missile Crisis: To the Brink of War*. Minneapolis, Minn.: Compass Point Books, 2006.

Cooper, Ilene. *Jack: The Early Years of John F. Kennedy*. New York: Dutton Children's Books, 2003.

Harrison, Barbara, and Daniel Terris. *A Twilight Struggle: The Life of John Fitzgerald Kennedy*. New York: Lothrop, Lee & Shepard, 1992.

Heiligman, Deborah. *High Hopes: A Photobiography of John F. Kennedy*. Washington, D.C.: National Geographic, 2003.

Hossell, Karen Price. *John F. Kennedy's Inaugural Speech*. Portsmouth, NH: Heinemann-Raintree, 2005.

Kennedy, John F. *Profiles in Courage*. New York: Harper, 1956.

Levine, Ellen S. *Freedom's Children: Young Civil Rights Activists Tell Their Own Stories*. New York: Putnam, 1993.

Levinson, Cynthia. *We've Got a Job: The 1963 Birmingham Children's March*. Atlanta, Ga.: Peachtree Books, 2011.

McWhorter, Diane. *A Dream of Freedom: The Civil Rights Movement from 1954 to 1968*. New York: Scholastic, 2004.

Sandler, Martin W. *Kennedy Through the Lens: How Photography and Television Revealed and Shaped an Extraordinary Leader*. New York: Walker & Company, 2011.

Tougas, Shelley. *Birmingham 1963: How a Photograph Rallied Civil Rights Support*. North Mankato, MN: Compass Point Books, 2011.

Recommended Websites

The single best place to find information, images, audio recordings, TV and news film footage, and lesson plans and suggestions for projects is the website of the John Fitzgerald Kennedy Presidential Library and Museum: www.jfk library.org.

Biographies of John F. Kennedy

www.jfklibrary.org/JFK/Life-of-John-F-Kennedy.aspx
www.whitehouse.gov/about/presidents/johnfkennedy

Biographies of Jacqueline Kennedy

www.jfklibrary.org/JFK/Life-of-Jacqueline-B-Kennedy.aspx
www.whitehouse.gov/about/first-ladies/jacquelinekennedy
   One is on the JFK Library site, the other is the official United States government biography on the White House website.

The History Channel

www.history.com/topics/john-f-kennedy
   A good overview of Kennedy's life and career with very good live links to people, historical events, and places.

Brainy Quote

www.brainyquote.com/quotes/authors/j/john_f_kennedy.html
www.brainyquote.com/quotes/authors/j/jackie_kennedy.html
   Many interesting words spoken and written by the president and first lady.

Kennedy's Career in the U.S. Navy

www.history.navy.mil/faqs/faq60-2.htm
   These pages on the official site of the U.S. Navy are not pretty to look at, but there is great information about PT boats and Kennedy's missions.

Warren Commission Report

www.archives.gov/research/jfk/warren-commission-report

   The full text of the report and images of all the exhibits that were presented.

Hear and Watch John F. Kennedy

www.presidency.ucsb.edu/medialist.php?presid=35

   A rich, fascinating list of 41 live links to Kennedy's radio remarks, TV interviews, inaugural address, speeches before the United Nations, addresses to the country about the Cuban missile crisis, and much more.

RECOMMENDED VIEWING

Cuban Missile Crisis: Three Men Go to War. Murray and Emer Reynolds, directors. DVD. PBS, 2012. 60 minutes, NR.

The JFK-Nixon Debates, 1960. DVD. Soundworks Recording Studio, 2011. 76 minutes, NR.

The Presidents: The Kennedys. DVD. PBS, 1992. 221 minutes, NR.

The Speeches Collection, Vol. 1. DVD. MPI Home Video, 2002. 240 minutes, NR. (Contains important speeches by John F. Kennedy, Martin Luther King Jr., Gerald Ford, and Ronald Reagan.)

The Search for Kennedy's PT-109. Peter Getzels, producer and writer. Warner, 2002. 60 minutes, NR.

BIBLIOGRAPHY

Anthony, Carl Sferrazza. *As We Remember Her: Jacqueline Kennedy Onassis, in the Words of Her Friends and Family*. New York: HarperCollins, 1997.

———. *The Kennedy White House: Family Life and Pictures, 1961–1963*. New York: Simon & Schuster, 2001.

Ballard, Robert D., and Michael Hamilton Morgan. *Collision with History: The Search for John F. Kennedy's PT 109*. Washington, D.C.: National Geographic, 2002.

Blaine, Gerald, and Lisa McCubbin. *The Kennedy Detail: JFK's Secret Service Agents Break Their Silence*. New York: Gallery Books, 2010.

Byrne, Paul J. *The Cuban Missile Crisis: To the Brink of War*. Minneapolis, Minn.: Compass Point Books, 2006.

Caro, Robert A. *The Passage of Power: The Years of Lyndon Johnson*. New York: Alfred A. Knopf, 2012.

Clarke, Thurston. *Ask Not: The Inauguration of John F. Kennedy and the Speech That Changed America*. New York: Henry Holt and Co., 2004.

Connally, Nellie, and Mickey Herskowitz. *From Love Field: Our Final Hours with President John F. Kennedy*. New York: Rugged Land, 2003.

Cooper, Ilene. *Jack: The Early Years of John F. Kennedy*. New York: Dutton Children's Books, 2003.

Corrigan, Jim. *The 1960s Decade in Photos: Love, Freedom, and Flower Power*. Berkeley Heights, N.J.: Enslow Publishers, 2010.

Dobbs, Michael. *One Minute to Midnight: Kennedy, Khrushchev, and Castro on the Brink of Nuclear War*. New York: Alfred A. Knopf, 2008.

Donovan, Robert. *PT-109: John F. Kennedy in World War II*. New York: McGraw-Hill, 2001 (40th anniversary edition).

Gitlin, Todd. *The Sixties: Years of Hope, Days of Rage*. New York: Bantam Books, 1987.

Goodwin, Doris Kearns. *The Fitzgeralds and the Kennedys: An American Saga*. New York: Simon & Schuster, 1987.

Harrison, Barbara, and Daniel Terris. *A Twilight Struggle: The Life of John Fitzgerald Kennedy*. New York: Lothrop, Lee & Shepard, 1992.

Heiligman, Deborah. *High Hopes: A Photobiography of John F. Kennedy*. Washington, D.C.: National Geographic, 2003.

Hill, Clint, and Lisa McCubbin. *Mrs. Kennedy and Me*. New York: Simon and Schuster, 2012.

Hossell, Karen Price. *John F. Kennedy's Inaugural Speech*. Portsmouth, NH: Heinemann-Raintree, 2005.

Kennedy, Caroline, and Michael Beschloss. *Jacqueline Kennedy: Historic Conversations on Life with John F. Kennedy*. New York: Hyperion, 2011.

Kennedy, John F. *Profiles in Courage*. New York: Harper, 1956.

Kennedy, Robert F., and Arthur M. Schlesinger Jr. *Thirteen Days: A Memoir of the Cuban Missile Crisis*. New York: W. W. Norton, 1969.

King, Martin Luther Jr. *A Testament of Hope: The Essential Writings and Speeches of Martin Luther King, Jr.* New York: Harper & Row, 1986.

Levine, Ellen S. *Freedom's Children: Young Civil Rights Activists Tell Their Own Stories*. New York: Putnam, 1993.

Levinson, Cynthia. *We've Got a Job: The 1963 Birmingham Children's March*. Atlanta, Ga.: Peachtree Books, 2011.

Lieberson, Goddard, ed. *John Fitzgerald Kennedy: As We Remember Him*. New York: Atheneum, 1965.

McWhorter, Diane. *Carry Me Home: Birmingham, Alabama: The Climactic Battle of the Civil Rights Revolution*. New York: Simon & Schuster, 2001.

Manchester, William. *One Brief Shining Moment: Remembering Kennedy*. Boston: Little, Brown and Company, 1983.

O'Reilly, Bill. *A Bold Fresh Piece of Humanity*. New York: Broadway Books, 2008.

O'Reilly, Bill, and Martin Dugard. *Killing Kennedy: The End of Camelot*. New York: Henry Holt & Company, 2012.

Panitt, Merrill, ed. *TV Guide*. "America's Long Vigil: A Permanent Record of What We Watched on Television from November 22 to 25, 1963." January 25, 1964.

Reeves, Richard. *Portrait of Camelot: A Thousand Days in the Kennedy White House*. New York: Abrams, 2010.

Rubin, Gretchen. *Forty Ways to Look at JFK*. New York: Ballantine Books, 2005.

Sandler, Martin W. *Kennedy Through the Lens: How Photography and Television Revealed and Shaped an Extraordinary Leader*. New York: Walker & Company, 2011.

Schlesinger, Arthur M. *A Thousand Days: John F. Kennedy in the White House*. Boston: Houghton Mifflin and Co., 1965.

Sorensen, Theodore C. *Kennedy*. New York: Harper & Row, 1965.

Tougas, Shelley. *Birmingham 1963: How a Photograph Rallied Civil Rights Support*. North Mankato, MN: Compass Point Books, 2011.

White, Theodore H. *The Making of the President, 1960*. New York: Atheneum Publishers, 1969.

Widmer, Ted, selector. *Listening In: The Secret White House Recordings of John F. Kennedy*. New York: Hyperion, 2012.

SOURCES

THIS BOOK REQUIRED BOTH primary and secondary source research. Much of the primary material came from interviews and reporting that the author has done over the years. In fact, he won a Press Club of Dallas Award for his reporting on the JFK assassination while at WFAA-TV. Extensive new information was gathered from a variety of law enforcement agents, in particular Richard Wiehl, the FBI agent assigned to investigate and debrief Marina Oswald after the shooting. We are grateful to Mr. Wiehl, who has never spoken before on the record about his findings.

Kennedy's Last Days is completely a work of nonfiction. It's all true. The actions of each individual and the events that took place really happened. The quotations are words people actually spoke. Those details are made possible in large part because JFK is a contemporary historical figure whose entire presidency was thoroughly documented by all manner of media.

The sheer volume of material available on the life and death of John F. Kennedy allowed for unexpected research delights when compiling the manuscript. Not only were there a number of first-person manuscripts that provided specific details about meetings, conversations, and events, but there are also numerous Internet videos of JFK's speeches and television appearances, which brought his words and voice to life during each writing day. For readers, taking the time to find and watch these will add immeasurably to learning more about John Kennedy.

To hear about life inside the Kennedy White House from Jackie herself, listen to *Jacqueline Kennedy: Historic Conversations on Life with John F. Kennedy*, a series of recordings she made not long after the assassination. It is remarkable to hear the honesty with which the former first lady speaks, particularly when she opens up about so many of the most famous and power-ful figures in the world at that time. As with her husband, her wit, warmth, and sheer presence are palpable.

The author owes a special debt to the team of Laurie Austin and Stacey Chandler at the Kennedy Library. No research request was too big or too small, and suffice it to say that it was quite a historical rush to receive, for instance, copies of John Kennedy's actual daily schedule, showing his precise location, the names of different people at various meetings, and the time each afternoon he slipped off to the pool or to "the Mansion." To read these schedules was to see the president's day come alive and gave a vivid feel for what life was like in the White House. When in Boston, a visit to the Kennedy Library is a must.

Special recognition must also go to William Manchester's *The Death of a President*, which was written shortly after the assassination and built around first-person interviews with almost everyone who was with JFK in Dallas on November 22, 1963. Manchester's work was written with the complete coop-eration of Jackie and the Kennedy family. The level of detail is fantastic for that very fact and proved invaluable as the ultimate answer to many questions when other resources conflicted with one another.

The backbone of this text are books, magazine articles, videos, the Warren Commission Report, and visits to places such as Dallas, Washington, and the Texas Hill Country. The author owes a debt of gratitude to the many brilliant researchers who have immersed themselves in the life and times of John Fitzger-ald Kennedy. Their works are listed in the bibliography.

These are some particularly helpful resources:

◇ The White House Museum website, which offers a fine map of the entire building, along with its history in words and pictures. The Kennedy Library's website is also a great source of detail on life in the White House.

◇ When it was necessary to know what the weather was on a specific day, the *Farmers' Almanac* for that year was very useful.

◇ The reader can go online and watch Jackie's excellent White House tour.

◇ The Kennedy Library's website has a feature that allows you to browse the *New York Times* by date. This provides much of the background information on the travels of the president, the atrocities in East Berlin, and other events.

◇ FBI special agent John Fain's recollection of Lee Harvey Oswald comes from Fain's Warren Commission testimony.

◇ Believe it or not, the *Mona Lisa*'s unveiling can be found on YouTube.

◇ The Warren Commission Report includes a solid summary on the history of presidential assassination and the need for a Secret Service. The Secret Service's own website shows this, too. Much of the behind-the-scenes information about the various agents and their details can be found in Clint Hill's fascinating *Mrs. Kennedy and Me*, and in Gerald Blaine's *The Kennedy Detail*.

◇ Many details about the freedom marchers came from *Washington Post* coverage the following day. Glenn Eskew's *But for Birmingham* and Diane McWhorter's *Carry Me Home* provide additional awesome detail. Shelley Tougas's *Birmingham 1963* speaks of how a single photograph changed so many minds.

◇ Martin Luther King Jr.'s entire "I Have a Dream" speech can be heard online at www.americanrhetoric.com.

◇ Special agent James Hosty's Warren Commission testimony provides the details about his visit to Ruth Paine.

◇ The Warren Commission Report and David Kaiser's *The Road to Dallas* provide unique insight into the days leading up to the assassination.

◇ There is still some question as to whether Oswald was actually the shooter whom Sterling Wood witnessed, since the owner of the shooting range swore he saw Oswald there on a completely different date. The fact that a lone man was seen firing a unique Italian rifle, however, is not in doubt.

◇ A wide range of websites and books were used to sift through the vast number of facts surrounding the assassination of John F. Kennedy. The timing, crowd descriptions, and arrival scene, as well as all other aspects of the shooting and drive to Parkland Hospital, are standard facts. However, the primary sources for specific conversations, private moments, and otherwise particular details are *The Death of a President*, the Warren Commission Report, *Mrs. Kennedy and Me*, Vincent Bugliosi's *Reclaiming History*, Robert Dallek's writings on JFK's medical woes and on the assassination itself, and, of course, the Zapruder film. The author watched it time after time after time to understand the sequence of events, and it never got less horrific—nor did the outcome ever change.

◇ Jackie's filmed newsreel thanking the nation for its sympathy can be found online, and her grief is still startlingly painful to watch.

INDEX

Page numbers in *italics* refer to maps and illustrations.

KENNEDY'S LAST DAYS

BONUS MATERIAL

A transcript of an interview with
BILL O'REILLY
by his publisher, Laura Godwin.

Laura Godwin (LG): As a young person, who did you look up to most?

Bill O'Reilly (BO): I didn't really have a lot of idols other than sports people. I was a big Willie Mays fan because I was raised in New York, and I remember my father taking me when I was a really little kid, maybe six years old, to the Polo Grounds to watch Willie, and so Willie was my man. And I liked the sports guys, because that was what I was interested in. I really didn't have any political people at all. I was just a little barbarian, running around playing games.

LG: What was your favorite thing about school?

BO: Nothing! I was the worst student in the world, and that's what *A Bold Fresh Piece of Humanity* was about. I—you know—I should say that I liked my classmates, and still keep in touch with many of them. Two of them actually work for me—guys that I met in the first grade. I did like my classmates. There were sixty of us at St. Brigid's School, but as far as the academics, I mean, I was really just an outlier on the whole deal. I liked to read. I was a good reader. And I was a big mouth. You know, in class, trying to get some laughs. But, academically, I really was just never a superstar until I got much older.

LG: And what about sports?

BO: I played everything. I played baseball and football, ice hockey, and basketball. So I was always sweating. I was always perspiring around the calendar.

LG: What was your favorite book when you were a kid?
BO: I liked the Hardy Boys books. The detective books? I read them all. In fact, I was reading them when I should have been doing other schoolwork. I loved those books. And then I read the Chip Hilton series, which was a sports guy. He was a sports thing. So I would read those, and my parents were *thrilled* because then I would shut up because I was reading, so they gave me as many books as I could handle. And very early on I became interested in history. I liked the action. I liked all the wars, and the conflicts, from Rome up until American history. So I started to read about that. I was reading a lot. As a kid, I was either playing sports or reading.

LG: What's your favorite childhood memory?
BO: Whew, that's a hard question. I mean, I don't want to be dodging a question, but—

LG: If nothing comes to mind, that's—
BO: Yeah, I mean there's just too many. I had a very independent childhood. There weren't a lot of events. We didn't have a lot of money. So there wasn't like, "oh, I went to Paris when I was ten." I mean, we went up to a lake in Vermont, and it was all right, but there wasn't anything stunning that I can point to basically because it was simple. It was a simple upbringing.

LG: Right, right. I mean, was it like family meals . . . ?
BO: Yeah, it was all that, but it wasn't like *Father Knows Best*. I mean it was like, "Do I have to eat this?" You know, it was a little turbulent.

LG: **What advice do you wish someone had given you when you were younger?**

BO: I think that you have to think before you act. You know, when you are raised in a working-class neighborhood, there's a lot of emotion, and people react—both children and adults—on emotion. And you know, if someone had pulled me aside—I don't know whether I would have listened—and said, "Look, you've got to, you know, count to fifteen or something before you hit the guy, you know, you don't really want to react emotionally. That doesn't usually work out well." So that would have been the piece of advice that I wish I had received.

LG: **Do you have any of the same hobbies now that you had when you were a kid?**

BO: Sure. I'm the same guy that I was when I was ten. I like sports and I read everything. And, you know, I socialize with the people I grew up with and, so, you know, I'm not a lot different than I used to be.

LG: **Do you still play any sports?**

BO: Yes, with my son. We play football, and I coach baseball, and we're out there skating. And, you know, I'm doing everything—swimming, diving. All of that. So that's a big part of my life.

LG: **Skating. I don't hear of a lot of New Yorkers who skate. And I'm a Canadian, so that was a big thing for us.**

BO: Yeah, I learned to skate when I was twelve and really liked playing hockey, and I was on the high school hockey team, so I don't play hockey now, but I do skate.

LG: **What was your first job? And what was your worst job?**

BO: First job was working at Carvel, for minimum wage. That's an ice cream stand. Had a blast. It was great. You know, I had to show up for work. I had to do the job. I was able to accomplish all of those things. Then we got free ice cream, and all the crew was close, and we had a lot of laughs, so that was a great experience. I'd say the worst job I had was painting houses. I started my own house-painting business to get money for college, and it was brutal! In the summer, we'd paint those houses on Long Island. We made a ton of money! It was great money, but boy was it hard, and that kind of solidified in my mind that I didn't want to be a working-class guy and have to do that every day of my life. So the money was great, and the experience was good, but the job was hell.

LG: Did you put yourself through school with that money?
BO: My father paid my tuition; I paid everything else.

LG: And how old were you at Carvel?
BO: Sixteen.

LG: What makes you laugh out loud?
BO: Clever comedians. Jonathan Winters was the best when I was growing up. There are a bunch of good guys now. Seinfeld is very clever. And then, you know, spontaneous stuff that happens. There is a segment by [Dennis] Miller on the *Factor*, and you know he'll come out with some outrageous stuff. When it catches you by surprise and it's quick and witty, I usually laugh.

LG: Do you have a favorite word?
BO: *Bloviate.*

LG: [Laughs] That's a good one. If you were stranded on a desert island, who would you want for company?
BO: Jesus.

LG: If you could travel in time, where would you go and what would you do?

BO: I think I would go to the American Revolution. I would be one of George Washington's aides, you know, one of the guys who was helping him out. I think that would be fascinating.

LG: If you were a superhero, what would your superpower be?

BO: Reading minds. That's the power you want.

LG: There's a superhero for sure. I'm surprised no one's done that. What would your readers be most surprised to learn about you?

BO: That I'm kind of boring off-camera. I'm not a party kind of guy, and I'm much "lower key" in private.

LG: What do you consider to be your greatest accomplishment?

BO: I think, you know, rising up from a fairly modest upbringing to write bestselling books and have the most-watched cable news program in the world. I mean, those are pretty good. We'll go with those.

LG: Those are pretty good, indeed. If you could meet President Lincoln today, what would you say to him?

BO: I'd congratulate him on being the best president ever. That would be number one. And then I would probably ask him a bunch of silly questions about why he did what he did, and how people treated him. You know, that kind of thing. Lincoln was a guy who didn't really have a lot of structure in his life but was very ambitious, and I would try to get into that. *Why were you so ambitious? Why did you want to leave Illinois and then go to Washington?* That kind of thing. What was driving him?

LG: What were you most surprised to learn while writing *Killing Lincoln*?

BO: How hated he was. I mean, they hated him on both sides. Confederates hated him and then a lot of people in the North hated him because they didn't really want slavery to be illegal. So boy, oh boy, he was the most hated man in the country at the time he was assassinated.

LG: What were you most surprised to learn while writing *Killing Kennedy*?

BO: Basically the Kennedy book was a very factual, disciplined look at how he was murdered. There were a couple of things that I couldn't get at that bothered me about people swirling around Oswald. But it was Oswald who did it. There's no doubt about it. I think the most surprising thing that I learned in that book was how heroic Jackie Kennedy was. I didn't really have a lot of regard for her before we began researching *Killing Kennedy*, and she really was a woman of courage and a woman who put other people before herself. I think the amount of respect I have for her now is a lot more than I had when I began the project.

LG: Do you have a favorite quote from President Kennedy?

BO: I think the "do for your country" is the best quote.

LG: Aside from President Kennedy and President Lincoln, who do you think are some of America's greatest heroes?

BO: Washington, no doubt. He was an *amazing* man. Jefferson intellectually was a hero, but not physically. We'll get into that somewhere down the line. I think Teddy Roosevelt was a hero. He was a little crazy, but he had a lot of vision and he did a lot of good things, especially on the environment. The people in World War Two—there were so many heroes there who were either killed or survived, but fighting this unbelievable evil, you know, a LOT of heroism in that war. The Vietnam vets who answered the call and tried to save these people in South Vietnam and got hammered from all sides. They were heroes. So, I mean, it's incalculable. We're a noble nation, America, and our history is dotted with heroes in almost every day that we've existed, so the line is just unlimited.

DISCUSSION QUESTIONS

PART ONE: The Making of a Hero
(Chapters 1–5, pages 1–43)

1. Explain why JFK's inauguration represented a new generation of Americans. During this time, where was Lee Harvey Oswald and what was he doing?

2. List the most interesting fact you learned about everyday life in 1961, the year JFK was elected president.

3. Explain why the death of JFK's oldest brother, Joe, is perhaps a larger influence on JFK's career in politics than his heroism at war.

PART TWO: The Making of a Leader
(Chapters 6–25, pages 45–156)

1. What is a typical day like for JFK while president? What did you find most interesting about a day in the life of an American president?

2. Despite many mistakes, how is the president received by the American public?

3. What is America's reaction to JFK's wife, Jackie? What role does she play in the White House?

4. Explain how close the U.S. and the Soviet Union come to all-out nuclear war. How is the crisis resolved? Do you think JFK handled the crisis well? Why?

5. On August 23, 1963, Martin Luther King Jr. delivers his famous "I Have a Dream" speech to 250,000 people in the shadow of the Lincoln Memorial. Explain JFK's reaction to this historic event based on his words and actions.

PART THREE: Dallas, Texas—November 1963
(Chapters 26–41, pages 157–239)

1. Name JFK's trusted advisers. Why do they urge JFK to cancel the "Big D" portion of his campaign trip in Texas?

2. Who is in charge of protecting JFK when he travels? How does this special agent prepare for JFK's Dallas visit?

3. List the rules that motorcades followed for both protection and visibility. How did the Kennedy motorcade through Dallas break these rules?

4. Describe Jackie's response to the tragic events. How does she try to protect JFK and his appearance to the public even in death?

5. How do important people and everyday citizens learn of the president's assassination? What was the most important news event that you remember hearing or reading about recently? How did you react?

PART FOUR: The Making of a Legend
(Chapters 42–43, pages 241–255)

1. How did the United States mourn the death of JFK? How did people show their respect?

2. List and briefly summarize each of the major legacies of JFK's short presidency.

Visit macmillan.com for the full Teacher's Guide!

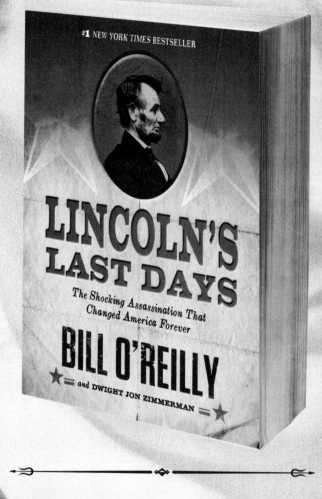

THE SHOCKING ASSASSINATION
that changed America forever...

#1 NEW YORK TIMES BESTSELLER

LINCOLN'S LAST DAYS

The Shocking Assassination That Changed America Forever

BILL O'REILLY
★ — *and* DWIGHT JON ZIMMERMAN — ★

LINCOLN'S LAST DAYS

is history like you've never read before.
Turn the page for a sneak peek.

SATURDAY, MARCH 4, 1865
Washington, D.C.

ABRAHAM LINCOLN, the man with six weeks to live, is anxious. The speech he is about to give is vital to the peace of the country. Since the Battle of Fort Sumter took place in South Carolina in April 1861, the United States has been a "house divided," locked in a civil war between the free North and the slaveholding South. Led by South Carolina, a total of eleven slaveholding states in the South have left the Union and formed a separate nation, the Confederate States of America. The states that seceded felt that maintaining the institution of slavery was essential to their economy and they were willing to leave the Union rather than outlaw slavery.

Lincoln tried to stop the states from leaving, but they refused his peaceful appeals. When Confederate troops fired on Union troops at Fort Sumter, Lincoln had no choice but to go to war. This civil war has not only divided the nation, it has also split countless families, pitting fathers against sons, and brothers against brothers. It is

Abraham Lincoln delivering his second inaugural address, March 4, 1865.
John Wilkes Booth is in the crowd to the right and above where the president stands.

a situation that even affects Lincoln's family. His wife, Mary Todd Lincoln, has relatives fighting for the Confederacy. Much blood—too much blood—has been shed in this terrible conflict. Lincoln sighs, hoping that it will end soon, and with the Union victorious.

Fifty thousand men and women are standing in pouring rain and ankle-deep mud to watch Abraham Lincoln take the oath of office to begin his second term.

Lincoln steps up to the podium and delivers an eloquent appeal for reunification in his second inaugural address.

"With malice toward none, with charity for all, with firmness in the right as God gives us to see the right, let us strive on to finish the work we are in, to bind up the nation's wounds, to care for him who shall have borne the battle and for his widow and his orphan, to do all which may achieve and cherish a just and lasting peace among ourselves and with all nations," the president says humbly. As he speaks, the sun bursts through the clouds, its light surrounding the tall and outwardly serene Lincoln.

Although Lincoln does not know this, 120 miles south of Washington, at the important railroad and communications center of Petersburg, Virginia, a siege that started in June 1864 is nearing its end. The Confederate Army of Northern Virginia, under the command of General Robert E. Lee, has been pinned in and around the city for more than 250 days by Union forces under the command of General Ulysses S. Grant. Lee knew if he didn't defend Petersburg, the road to the Confederate capital of Richmond would be wide open. The capture of Richmond by Union troops would be a powerful symbolic victory, telling everyone that the end of the Confederacy was near. So Lee ordered his army to stay, dig trenches, and fight.

But now, in April 1865, Lee's army is weak. At this point, if Lee remains and continues to defend Petersburg, his forces will be destroyed by Grant's Army of the Potomac, which grows stronger in men and guns with each passing week. Lee knows that Grant is preparing for an overwhelming attack. Lee plans to have his army slip out of Petersburg and escape south to the Carolinas before that happens. If he succeeds, Lincoln's prayer for a reunified United States of America may never be answered. America will continue to be divided into a North and a South, a United States of America and a Confederate States of America.

———•◦×◦•———

Lincoln's inaugural speech is a performance worthy of a great dramatic actor. And indeed, one of America's most famous actors stands just yards away as the president speaks. Twenty-six-year-old John Wilkes Booth is inspired by the president's words—though not in the way Lincoln intends.

The president has ambitious plans for his second term in office. Ending the war and healing the war-torn nation are Lincoln's overriding ambitions. He will use every last bit of his trademark determination to see these goals realized; nothing must stand in his way.

But evil knows no boundaries. And a most powerful evil—in the person of John Wilkes Booth and his fellow conspirators—is now focused on Abraham Lincoln.

John Wilkes Booth.

January 17, 1961

The inaugural is a beginning an end
as well as a beginning — Today we are
on 35,000 persons.
turned on the all these Presidents's
and of from when 3 are with eyes
the three living are in the weekday and
all those & the men who stood in
this same place, took the same
oath, made the same commitment.
to the preservation of my American constitution and
its promises because there is a resoluteness
that we have made today.
would in interest in which we

here are a young people — as
an new Republic — but they the can
are old — as least as in holy's
for behind by them are immense.
we know that they can
my that this are descended
for Revolutionaries — & standor successors